C000292076

The Crystal Healer

To Hilary
with very best Witches ☆
Marianna Sheldrake
10.8.12

The Crystal Healer

A GUIDE TO UNDERSTANDING CRYSTALS AND THEIR HEALING GIFTS

MARIANNA SHELDRAKE

Index compiled by Lyn Greenwood

SAFFRON WALDEN
THE C.W. DANIEL COMPANY LIMITED

First published in Great Britain in 1999
by The C.W. Daniel Company Limited
1 Church Path, Saffron Walden,
Essex, CB10 1JP United Kingdom

Reprinted 2000
© Marianna Sheldrake 1999

ISBN 9781846042478

The author has asserted her rights under the Copyright Design and
Patent Act 1988 (and under any comparable provision of any comparable law
in any jurisdiction whatsoever) to be identified as the author of this work.

So far as may legally effectively be provided no liability of any kind or nature
whatsoever, whether in negligence, under statute, or otherwise, is accepted
by the author or the publishers for the accuracy or safety of any of the
information or advice contained in, or in any way relating to any part of the
content, of this book.

All rights reserved. No part of this publication may be reproduced, stored
in a retrieval system, or transmitted in any form or by any means, electronic,
mechanical, photocopying, recording, or otherwise, without the prior
permission of the copyright holder.

Produced in association with Book Production Consultants plc,
25–27 High Street, Chesterton, Cambridge CB4 1ND
Designed and typeset by Ward Partnership, Saffron Walden, Essex

The Random House Group Limited supports The Forest Stewardship
Council (FSC®), the leading international forest certification organisation.
Our books carrying the FSC label are printed on FSC® certified paper.
FSC is the only forest certification scheme endorsed by the leading
environmental organisations, including Greenpeace. Our
paper procurement policy can be found at
www.randomhouse.co.uk/environment

Printed and bound in Great Britain by Clays Ltd, St Ives PLC

Contents

Illustrations

Introduction

I have lost count of the number of people who have asked me the leading question, 'How do I become a healer?' The answer is deceptively simple – you must first believe in your own abilities. I truly believe that anyone has the potential to heal another, but the most difficult obstacle in their path is themselves. With some, it is scepticism; with others, it is a lack of self-assurance and with most, it is the misconception that healing requires the aid of some frightening level of magic or mysticism. Let me be clear on this point. *I believe that healing is one of the most natural processes that we humans can share with each other.*

After half a lifetime spent in the healing arts, I felt that the greatest contribution I could make, in return for the marvellous experiences I had been privileged to enjoy, would be to attempt to 'lift the veil' a little and help people to see the nature of their own relationship with the universe – and the powers that flow from it. This book is my effort to help newcomers to the crystal experience by rolling back some of the mystery and superstition that have shrouded the subject for so long. It is also intended to provide experienced practitioners with a useful, practical reference work on the most commonly used crystals and some of the techniques I have found helpful.

One of the great good fortunes of my life has been the time spent amongst other healers both in my work with healing 'circles' and through the shop I have in Glastonbury with my husband, Brian. We have travelled together across the world, speaking to groups and meeting dedicated healers. We meet healers, both experienced and novice, when they come through our shop. No matter which sphere of life they might move in, I am always struck by the simplicity of belief that we all share. I have met healers who have no real religious beliefs at all, other than a simple acceptance of a supreme intelligence, and I have met deeply devoted Christian healers. They all share a concept of 'unconditional love' that unites them and motivates their selfless devotion. I have long since reached the conclusion that 'belief systems' are simply mechanisms that allow us to contact or gain access to the terrific energies that abound throughout the cosmos – and it is these energies that heal . . . not us.

On a recent tour through New Mexico and Arizona we were introduced to a revered elder of the Lakota people called Hollis Littlecreek. We met at a talk he was giving and he asked us to visit with him the next day. We spent a day with him, sharing insights and ideas, and he honoured us with a detailed description of some ancient beliefs shared by a number of native American nations – including his close friends, the mysterious 'Hopi'. He has spent a number of years working with them towards a wider understanding of the ancient 'tribal prophecies' especially the Hopi prophecy that talks of a 'Rainbow of Understanding' whereby the Red Man and the White Man share their ancient knowledge and bring about a new movement of respect and healing for 'Mother Earth'.

Those who work towards this goal are known as 'Rainbow Warriors'. Hollis believes that crystals are an integral part of the lifecycle and that understanding this relationship is an essential first step towards crystal healing. I offer his thoughts for your consideration:

The plant takes nourishment from the minerals of Mother Earth. We eat the plant and survive. Some of the plants have to go through another transformation, so that their properties will not hurt our body. Animals eat these plants and then we eat those animals and survive. Ultimately, however, the plants, the animals and ourselves die and the bodies return to Mother Earth. In a few million years (no time at all for a planet) the bodies have become minerals again. And so we see that even in the physical world we live forever. We are a wonderfully harmonious balance between the spiritual energy that comes from the Great Spirit and the physical body that comes from Mother Earth. This is the real 'Circle of Life'.

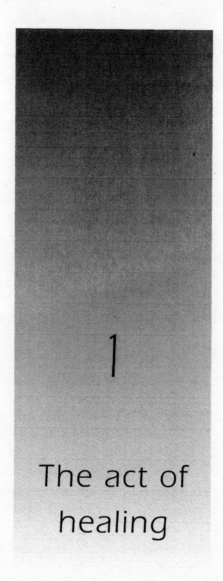

1

The act of
healing

Probably the most important prerequisite for someone
approaching crystal healing for the first time is an open mind.
Like you, I am always wary of anyone prefacing their information with that phrase. But, in this case, it's perfectly true.
There is a quaint comparison that I remind myself of whenever
I take a look at something new. *A closed mind is like a closed parachute
– absolutely useless and, at the wrong time, potentially fatal.* Whatever
beliefs have brought you this far through your life are not
in question. I have found that the concepts surrounding the

energies of crystals are perfectly compatible with just about any
beliefs. This is because crystal energy is a manifestation of
science – the emerging field of 'subtle energies' – and I hold the
view that science and spirituality are not incompatible at all.

The act of healing itself is a relatively small part of a cosmic
mechanism. We do know, from physics, that everything – and I
do mean *everything* – needs energy to exist. Now, energy is quite
an amazing concept. It cannot be seen, felt or measured. Only
the *effects* of energy can be quantified. Cosmologists seem to
agree at least about one facet of energy – it is constant and ever
present. In fact, there are many who go further and would
maintain that all the energy sources that man has ingeniously
'invented' have only been manipulations of the existing energy
of the universe. Nuclear power is just one example. Scientists
found that they could produce awesome energy flows by
manipulating atoms. But hasn't the universe been demonstrating
its own power of manipulation by the creation of stars and
galaxies since time began? As a species, man has been extremely
inventive in the manipulation of his environment, but still he
has only arrived at a point where he is just starting to see how
much he has yet to learn.

There is an incredible energy source that flows through the
entire cosmos. It seems to have existed since the beginning
of our universe and, in fact, may well be a residue from the
original energy source that created all universes. I have no
intention, here, of entering further into the debate regarding the
origins of this energy which I am contented to leave to the
theoretical physicists and cosmologists. Suffice it to say that
the existence of this 'super energy' is the basis for all spiritual
healing – of which crystal healing is a significant part.

At this point, I should make it perfectly clear that the healer is
not the source of the healing energy – simply a conductor. A
healer spends much of their time refining or attuning their

receptive and conductive abilities. The healer aims to place themselves in the position of drawing the super energy into them and passing it through their own body and into the body of the recipient. The role of the crystal is to act – sometimes as an amplifier, sometimes as a focusing lens – in channelling the energy flow. The super energy itself is visualised in many different ways according to the beliefs of the individual. Some see this power as radiating from God, whilst others simply visualise the power itself as the source of all energy. Whatever your beliefs, how you visualise this power is not nearly as important as the fact that you *do* visualise it. The capacity for visualisation is the strongest ability we have and it's the key to any aspect of spirituality. There is much truth in the axiom 'What we can imagine – we can achieve'.

The mind is another area of deep mystery, but psychologists agree that mental imagery is incredibly strong. Before we can achieve anything new we have to be able to 'see' ourselves achieving it. The biggest difference between a successful person and an under-achiever is in their own self-image. To successfully heal another we must be able to see the energy flowing through ourselves, see it entering the recipient and see the disease healing. Make no mistake – visualisation is hard work at first. But, with practice, it will quickly become second nature and you will find it difficult to remember a time when you weren't able to see clearly. Practice is the only way, but be careful. We are often told that 'practice makes perfect'. This is not true. Practice only makes *permanent*. Remember – only the practice of *perfection* can make perfect. Take great care in the early stages because it is here that you will build the habits of healing that will stay with you for life.

All living things have a natural tendency towards wellness. When left to its own devices, nature drives us towards the things needed by the body. How many times do we wonder at the strange cravings of pregnant women for exotic foods for example? It's not that they have suddenly developed inexplicable tastes for such delights as pickles and custard or chocolate spread on garlic bread. It is simply that the body seems to know what nutrients it needs and, more strangely, where to find them. The body's needs, however, are temporary and such cravings only last for as long as they are needed. After the pregnancy, the mother's habitual tastes soon return. Most illnesses are like this and medicine doesn't seem to offer a satisfactory explanation.

I have found that someone who is troubled will naturally gravitate towards a crystal or mineral that can help them. This is their own 'inner healer' asserting itself. The sad thing is that, in this age of technology and achievement, we find it so difficult to accept such natural concepts as an 'automatic built-in systems monitor'. The body, though, has not lost this ancient ability and it can often prove to be far more reliable than our intellect. When we offer healing to someone we first have to try and connect with their body's own repair system and determine where their weaknesses lie. It has often amazed me just how much information the body can give us – if we know how to look. The next step towards healing is to help the subject (or patient) to understand and visualise the problems for themselves. Then we are able to complete the circuit by drawing the super energy into ourselves and focusing the flow on the subject. That, in its simplest form, is how healing works. But with this understanding there comes a serious responsibility.

In recent years there has been much written about the power of positive thinking – if one believes strongly enough, a change will take place. Personally, I think there's a great deal of truth in the concept, but crystal healing involves much more than that. It is more than faith healing – the concept that if one's faith is strong enough and unfaltering one will be healed. My natural curiosity has led me to examine many of these theories and I'm afraid most of them crumbled under closer scrutiny, experimentation and the cold light of day. My logical mind will not give in, however, to the rather disconcerting rate of growth in what I have come to call 'the pink fluffy cloud chasers' who profess every thing to be 'wonderful', kiss your crystals and want to buy instant spirituality at three dollars a bottle (two for only five dollars). Somewhere underneath all the confusion there is a natural process happening that is accessible to everyone and is a mixture, if you will, of 'science and magic'. After all – *magic is only a science yet to be explored.*

Perhaps I can explain how I came to understand crystal healing and my study of a subject that, from a scientific standing point is still shrouded in mystery. My personal relationship with crystals has led me along a dual path. I have, and continue to have, a fascinating journey of exploration as I explore the amazing energies of the human body and the ways in which they interact with the energy patterns of minerals. But further beyond that, it may be the thrill of occasionally adding something to the fast growing body of scientific knowledge in the newly recognised field of subtle energies which is enough to make one feel part of evolution instead of an accidental spectator.

Twenty two years ago I took a course in pyramid selling. There was a lot of promotion, at the time, of mind over matter so I took a course myself, hoping to learn about empowerment and the achievements that were allegedly possible to gain from it. I suppose looking back the thing that frightened me most about the whole movement was that no one was teaching responsibility. We were being taught to look the prospective customer straight in the eye, to be assertive, to nod our head to affirm we sincerely mean what we said, and believe unreservedly in what we were selling. To relentlessly pursue and follow up until Mrs X bought the product – even though she neither required or needed it. At the end of the day all that mattered were targets, results and who achieved the most. The best in his or her field. Competition. Conscience never came into it. It didn't matter that Mrs X didn't want the product, could not afford the product, or had no use for the product. What mattered was that your will to make her buy the product was far greater then hers in attempting to resist. This concept was probably the most important breakthrough for me coming to terms with healing. Mind over matter, one person's energy totally focused on bending another person's energy and willpower. This, I began to realise, could be considered a form of magic.

But what of the universal laws of karma and the laws relating to cause and effect. No one addressed these issues. When I posed this question some smarmy, smooth talking lecturer reiterated as if I were some innocent who had just woken up from my cradle. 'Who cares about karma, cause and effect, lady, we are talking targets, quotas and checks.' I knew about cause and effect right then because he made me feel positively sick. I completed the course because I felt I should learn to have more control over my life, it was a lesson I took a long time to learn.

When I was a child my father had a sales round and I remember, one particular week, going with him. He came back to the car, where I had been waiting for him, overjoyed. He had sold a beautiful, and quite expensive, stair carpet. However, the following week when he called to collect the first payment on the carpet, he was in for a surprise. The gentleman met him at the door with a broad grin. 'I'll take my hat off to you son' he said, 'as a salesman you're the tops, but I suppose you never noticed – I live in a bungalow'. My father had been so concerned with trying to make his living, by making that big sale, that he'd totally failed to consider if the item was of any use to the customer. They both saw the funny side of it and it later became one of my father's favourite stories. However, I learnt, through

my father's eyes, his enormous sense of guilt and unpro-
fessionalism. He had put his needs before the customer's.
Every now and then your conscience trips you up and exposes
a facet of your true nature. You don't always like what you
see. My father gave up that job not long after the incident
because the terrific pressure to achieve targets was altering his
true nature – and he wasn't comfortable with it. I'm proud to say
he still has a conscience and I have a lot of respect for him
because of it.

It was the concept of 'winners and losers' that fascinated me
and drew me into studying this relationship at great length. It
bothered me greatly and I believe that, on reflection, what I had
witnessed as a child with my father was significant to me. It
had shown me balance. My father had refused to allow his
integrity to be bought. Looking at this objectively, I think it was
the right decision for him and, I'll bet, it added years to his life.
The stress of being in a position which makes you uncomfort-
able works against your nature and results in agitation. The
unsettled mind sends out confused signals and the body reacts at
its weakest point.

I have noticed this same effect on people I have helped over
the years with healing. Many who have been continuously in a
position of submission or suppression suffer on the weakest part
of their body. If you were to gauge the energy output of a high
powered sales person closing an important sale, his vibration
would have to be accelerated and positive. On the other hand,
someone who has just lost a deal, into which they had put a lot
of time and effort, that would even reflect on their position and
salary, would have a very low energy output and vibration. One
day I am sure doctors will have a machine that will measure
these subtle energy fields accurately and determine which of
the body's energy centres have the lowest output. Then, even
though these may not directly relate to the symptoms presented

by the physical body, it would show areas where the aura or the emotional body is under attack – and where to begin the healing process.

So what, you may ask, has this to do with crystals? After all any good counsellor would reach the same conclusion. All crystals have a vibration. Not necessarily one that is obvious – a subtle one. And, just as like attracts like, one vibration recognises another of the same frequency. That is quite simply the science, or magic, of crystal healing. We all feel more comfortable with people of a like mind. Why? Because we have more in common. A slow, sluggish energy centre on the human body, whether one can see and feel it or not, will be instantly attracted to the slow, low energy of a crystal or mineral of the same vibration. Likewise, a positive, vibrant energy centre on the human body would draw toward a crystal or mineral with that same output. To take that theory a step further, an overexcited, hyperactive metabolic system that oozes imbalance would be drawn to a crystal or mineral vibrating at a similar frequency.

Through so many years of working with people in these fields, I've developed a clear picture of their sceptical yet strangely inquisitive behaviour towards healers – and in particular to crystal energies. I would play a guessing game with myself each time someone new came into the shop. Their choice of crystals or minerals told me much about them and their needs. Most believed they were choosing a stone according to their tastes, which of course is another thing entirely. What I noticed, time and time again, was that when they started talking – if they were honest enough to admit to their ailment – their choice in crystals would uncannily match the energy output of that area. Very often they would not say exactly what was wrong with them, but would put their hand on the appropriate area. The crystal chosen seemed always to relate to that area. Intuition on their behalf or coincidence? I happen to believe that the human body in all its complexities has an in-built emergency system of self survival. It appears to be able to put out a 'distress signal' almost *before* the ailment occurs. If only we were able to read it more clearly we could take greater evasive measures. So the body, through identification, is sending out a distress signal and we have purchased that crystal. What does one do with it? How can it help?

I believe what has happened is an identification of that unbalanced energy centre and, by having that crystal near you, an exchange of energy takes place. The amount put out is balanced by the amount sent back. This stabilises that centre. At this point it is not necessarily getting any better – but neither is it getting any worse. Having maintained a point of equilibrium, the next stage is to identify the cause of the imbalance and rectify it. Unlike conventional medicine, popping a few pills may not be the answer. We all want instant results but, as much as we may want our bodies to behave like well oiled machines, the reality is that they are flesh and blood and, as such, are affected by outside influences – particularly our emotions. However, this does not mean control over one's emotions automatically ensures good health because to suppress one's emotions can be extremely dangerous. It means that we must confront our emotions and unravel what we are feeling and, often more importantly, why we are feeling it. We can very often help ourselves to better health through understanding ourselves. Balance within our mental state leads to balance within our body. I realise that there is nothing new to this concept – but it is essential that we grasp this relationship firmly if we are to 'heal' others. The exact mechanisms by which this phenomenon occurs has been the subject of years of research (and acres of rainforest paper). I have to admit that I am no more able to explain these mechanisms than anyone else, and I find myself deeply sceptical of those who say that they can. However,

I am certain of their existence and have learned to make use of them quite effectively. You do not need to know the complete mechanics of the internal combustion engine in order to drive your car. You do, however, need to know where the ignition is – and where to put in the fuel. The starting and sustaining. Trying to understand our mind, and why we think and feel as we do, is like running the car. Continually balancing ourselves – 'this has happened, how do I feel about it' – is the equivalent of topping up the fuel tank. Just like tuning the car engine – we need to sustain balance.

Once we have addressed the cause, our energy centres start to readjust. There is movement and we will be drawn to a different crystal with a higher vibration. We may need to keep this crystal in our pocket and use it like a worry bead'. A constant reminder of why it is there and a trigger to the defence mechanism to step-up its vigilance when there is a danger of attack. You may need to be still and try to meditate with the crystal or sleep with it under the pillow. The simple act of admiring the crystal for its beauty sends out a subconscious love emotion and this is all that is needed to begin the process of restoring one's balance. A wave of communication is sent out through having cracked open, even if only slightly, a deeply hidden sensitive side to your nature which is extremely receptive to the universal energies that feed our soul.

We have many ailments today that are blamed on the society and times in which we live. More stress-related illnesses and cases of depression than at any other time in history. Wouldn't it be a medical achievement, then, if it were possible to prevent these symptoms from developing into more serious diseases by detecting and removing them at source. The success rate with crystal healing seems to be related to the level of the patient's own participation. Firstly, the patient feels they are taking part in the diagnosis giving them a role to play as a researcher of their very own ailment, and thereby achieving a greater under-standing of themselves. Secondly, they realise that they have a role to play in the healing itself. As they learn more about themselves and their lives they realise that they have choices, whether it be a crystal for their ailment or making a decision about the rest of their life. They are learning a radical lesson about taking *responsibility* for themselves.

Although healing with crystals can not promise an immediate cure, my research has led me to believe that what it does offer is a *permanent* cure. It dissolves the negative energy that is working against the system by identifying it and eradicating it – helped by the will and intent not only of the healer but of the patient themselves. Once the patient understands why they feel or act as they do they stand a much better chance of healing themselves. Crystals and minerals are an integral part of this healing process because the patient no longer feels so totally helpless and alone with their illness. They feel they are taking control of the illness and the responsibility for its eradication. Many times I have witnessed a complete 'overnight' change in a patient after just one healing. Their attitude is more positive. Their poise becomes more confident and erect as they hold themselves stronger. They rediscover their dignity. There are many who respond really well to alternative healing because they are allowed to feel part of their own 'cure'.

There are, of course, cases where little can be done, either by the medical profession or otherwise. For some it is simply that their time has come and the best one can do for them is comfort them and give them the encouragement they need to get them through their toughest hours. Some just need somewhere to go where they are not made to feel guilty about their feelings and can face up to them before letting them go. Somewhere to talk to 'like minded souls' who will not judge them or hurry them – for what is time when you are facing the inevitable.

What to expect
on a visit to a crystal healer

If someone comes to me for a consultation on crystal healing –
and it is their first time – I have a huge amount of respect for
them. To ask for help can sometimes be the hardest thing they
have ever done. It is almost like admitting that they are at a loss.
Sadly, because of ignorance and superstition, alternative answers
are usually only turned to when all else has failed them. For this
reason I take what I do extremely seriously. The very credibility
of alternative therapies is in our hands. The only way we have of
being respected is to show respect for our work – and respect for
those who come to us for help. There are enough people out
there who are only too happy to dismiss the energies of crystals
as just another growing body of the 'pink fluffy cloud brigade'.

There are as many situations as there are crystals. I may well
use different crystals or techniques on two people suffering from
the same complaint. No two people are the same and, because
their path in life has a large role to play in their ailment, it would
not be fair to treat them the same. Here are some examples
drawn from cases I have worked on. You will quickly realise
how versatile the healer has to be . . .

A lady came to the healing centre who was extremely quiet.
She hardly said a word and, although obviously there for a
healing, she was not prepared to enter into any dialogue. Her
face was expressionless and as I worked on her auric body, just
my hands above her, I realised she was taking a huge amount of
energy into the area of the heart chakra. As I moved my hands
away there was a terrific force pulling my hands back to that
centre. I continued to channel energy for her, allowing her to
take what was required before moving on. The other area of note
was around the head. Here the energy was very dissipated and in

some way was trying to make a form. I felt it was re-structuring. I decided to work with some Prehnite as this has the ability to bring light into dark places, to connect one to the grid of the universe so to speak. The chaotic energy around the head was rather disconcerting and while it struggled to reform into some kind of structure the physical body was left almost entirely unprotected. This resulted in the patient feeling totally cut off. This would also explain why there had been no rapport between us. I stroked the Prehnite through her aura, around the head, taking it upward and outward. It felt a bit like untangling a lot of fluffy wool. It was fragile and soft. The pace was interesting too. It seemed to slow down very gradually as I worked. When the energy field felt calmer I began to work on the heart chakra itself. This is a very sensitive chakra to work on and I decided to use a Rose Quartz wand. I would normally tell people to take the wand and use it by stroking towards the heart. However, there is always the exception and this was such a case. The heart centre was very heavy and weighed down. It would not have benefited from having more work to do. I started at the top of the heart and worked carefully up towards the head, feeling for any minor adjustments that may occur. I then worked from the bottom of the heart down towards the solar plexus, again noting any changes. I did the same on the left and right side, only a few strokes but a very subtle energy change occurred and I felt that was enough. The lady took some deep breaths and I noticed she was filling her lungs; it was as if they had been only working at half their normal capacity and now they were released and she could breathe more deeply. I returned to the top of the lady's head and placed my hands gently on her shoulders to let her know the healing was over. She took a moment as if she seemed to be coming out of a long sleep. It was quite a few moments before she seemed to be fully conscious and able to focus.

She slowly moved from the couch onto a chair and took a drink of water. She remained very quite and I went over the healing with her, explaining what I had been doing. At first she didn't seem interested but her eye was caught by a small piece of Peacock Ore. I handed it to her and after a moment she asked what it was for. She had an extremely graceful manner and every action was very correct and proper. I told her that from my own experience Peacock Ore has the ability to allow one to come to terms with grief, allowing one to let go and move on. It is very good with the negative energies that surround feelings of guilt and seems to accept our human imperfections. It almost gives one the permission to parcel up the experience and put it down. The lady listened thoughtfully and after a minute she said 'I think I'd like one of those'.

We moved into the kitchen and I made her a cup of tea, she spoke to one of the other healers there. I thought that was progress in itself. Before she left, she told me she was coming to terms with losing her husband. He had been her whole life and she had always put him first. Now she was feeling confused. You could see that within her grief, which was total, there were also feelings of release and freedom. She felt guilty for having the feeling that now she could do so many things she never had time for before. I have never seen that lady since then and that is how it should be. She had come to terms with her grief and I knew, in time, she would be moving on.

Another healing I gave to a lady who had had a number of problems surrounding the base chakra. She was undergoing treatment for cervical cancer, following a year of uncertainty, unsatisfactory smear tests etc., and understandably was distressed. There is one crystal in particular that I have found to display remarkable abilities in removing unwanted growths, warts and such. However, it has to be used with care for the same crystal also works on making things more than they may otherwise be in their natural state. The magical ingredient is the Moon cycle and it is something that farmers have known and used for years. The Full Moon to the New Moon is called the Waning Moon and is a time of recession, regression and basically a time to get rid of the unwanted. The New Moon through to the Full Moon is the balance, the opposite. It is called the Waxing Moon and is a time of growth, fertility and healing, a time of regenerating and recharging the physical body.

This crystal I used is called Ametrine and is a combination of Amethyst and Citrine. It is also a combination of the two energies associated with each. The only other crystal I have noticed that has the ability to be both male and female, negative and positive and that you need to be aware of the Moon cycle is Tourmaline. I have a pendant made up of a large Ametrine point which I wear in times of negativity and when I feel under attack. It works well as a shield of armour and always makes me feel more positive. However, what I have noticed is that when wearing it at the time of the Waning Moon I am at ease with it all the time. When wearing it at the time of the Waxing Moon it works well on 'bad hair days' but on normal days it makes me feel very hyperactive and extra sensitive.

I used this crystal on the woman over two months, twice in each cycle during the Waning Moon, and the first time she returned to the hospital they told her that her condition had stabilised and at the following visit they informed her that the condition was in remission. That didn't mean she was clear, it just meant that they would keep checking on her and see what the changes would be over the coming months. I thought this was very positive and, although it wasn't practical for her to continue to visit me due to the miles of distance, we worked out a plan for her to continue to work on herself.

A few years ago I was consulted by a man suffering badly from a frozen shoulder. He was a long distance lorry driver and had been referred to me by a colleague. He was a lovely man who came for a healing and spent the entire day. He had a million questions about who he was, where he was going and how his beliefs were constantly changing. He wanted to know everything – about every path. I, with a companion in the same room, worked on his aura first and did the customary balancing. Then he sat up and I worked on his back, down his spine and eventually along both of his arms. The confusion he felt about his identity was being carried in his frame – throughout the length of his spine. Every part of this area was tight, locked up, and tense. He spent a great deal of time on his own and so had plenty of time to think. He had no one of 'like-mind' to talk to and no one to share ideas with. Unable to unravel the mysteries on his own and, experiencing aspects that had seemed peripheral to him before, he had gradually felt more and more alone – and had 'closed down'. The spine is a well-known repository for stress and, not helped by his job which allowed little room for exercise, I could feel the spine beginning to compress down and lock up.

First I worked with a piece of Rutilated Quartz. I began by opening the aura around the stress points on the frame. I took the crystal up through the energy field toward the crown chakra and away from the body. I used long strokes taking my full arm's length. At the end of each stroke I shook the crystal to awaken the energy around the man. Then I repeated the same action along his shoulders and down his arms – always reaching outward. Once the energy field around the man had been opened up a little it gave me the opportunity to work on the frozen shoulder. I used a Tourmalinated Quartz wand for this and, channelling the energy from source through my body and into the wand, I was able to hit the precise point needed to destroy the energy block. This healing was more difficult because of the resistance the man had built up. The energy was going through his shoulder and, as the negative energy dissipated, it was being transferred directly into my open hand behind his shoulder. I was receiving the most painful cramp I had ever experienced in one place, so excruciating that it was bending my arm. At this point, the man said he could feel a sense of warmth going into his shoulder and the pain was leaving him. I had to use all my powers of concentration to ground this negative charge as quickly as possible. I didn't want to be left with his waste product. I controlled my breathing and began visualising with all the will and intent I could muster; it was truly a battle of wills. Eventually the pain released and I felt it drain out of my body. The man had not stopped talking through the last crucial few minutes. He jumped up feeling full of vitality. I, on the other hand, was feeling drained and thinking to myself 'I wish he would be quite for a few minutes'. I needed to finish the closing down of the healing and disconnect myself from his energy field.

Later, over the customary cup of tea, he told me that he had found a lady friend some months back with whom he had shared a relationship. Even though it had lasted only a few months, they had been experiencing some progress along a – shall we say 'magikal path'. They had finished on bad terms and by all accounts she had become a pretty egotistical character wishing to become some sort of 'high priestess' and needing a suitable 'high priest'. Evidently he didn't measure up and she had found someone else to fill the role, leaving my patient in the role of 'apprentice slave'. He had felt that she harboured negativity towards him and was 'working' against him. It was around this time that his complaint had first started.

Now I know that a lot of us have trouble believing in such concepts as 'spells' and 'malevolent thought-forms' but I share Shakespeare's view in this – '*There are more things in Heaven and Earth*' etc. etc. In fact, I believe that, in such cases as this, the most important opinion is that of the recipient. I have found that if someone believes themselves to be the victim of such 'magik', it's effects are only too real.

This had been a particular difficult healing, but because of my experience in dealing with malevolent energies, it had resulted in a successful conclusion. However, I know of healers who have taken on the 'entities' themselves and have had trouble dealing with them. This patient was a genuinely nice guy who had got a little lost. He deserved something better and, after the day spent together at the healing centre, he thanked us all and departed. He phoned regularly for a few months telling us of his progress and occasionally needing support until eventually he had the confidence to 'fly solo' again. Cases like this leave me with an immense feeling of doing something worthwhile at the healing centre and it is good for everyone there to feel part of that.

My time has to be divided between my many activities and I am not always in the healing centre or the shop beneath. But this is where I have spent most my working life, with the general public, and I owe a lot to the rich tapestry of characters that have come to us for help of one sort or another. Often they do not have the courage to inquire about healing openly and will 'sidle up' and start conversations hoping to gently broach the subject. If they only knew how much I learn from each of them and how grateful I have become for the gifts that enable me to offer them help.

Frequently I find people will come in and, being their first encounter with crystals, they may be sceptical or wary. But their desire to find some help or a cure will often give them enough courage to wander around and enquire about the energy of crystal healing. I do feel for them because many feel that the medical profession has failed them or let them down. They may feel that they're a casualty of not conforming to an ailment that can be treated by drugs or established surgical procedures. There is a stage between feeling that something is wrong and knowing something is wrong that requires medical treatment. Usually one waits until the latter. As they cautiously read the write ups about the qualities of the crystals some will laugh at their attributes, others will pick them up and hold them not aware as to how they are supposed to use them. One thing I find is quite common, people get embarrassed because they can not comprehend how a simple 'piece of rock' can help or heal them. A question I am continually asked is 'What can you recommend for depression?' This, on the face of it, is a reasonable question, but things are rarely that simple are they? To break the ice I would sometimes reply 'A two week holiday in the Bahamas' or 'A candlelit dinner for two in a posh restaurant'. But, once a rapport has been established, we usually begin to deal with the issue at hand. One example of this is a smartly dressed man who came in – briefcase in one hand, mobile phone in the other – with exactly this question. Obviously a 'man on the move' and in a hurry, he was adamant that he had no time to make his way upstairs to the healing centre. What he really wanted was to buy a crystal for a couple of pounds and let it solve all his problems. After all, he was far to busy to deal with them. I got him into conversation and asked him what he felt was causing the depression. Depression is multi-faceted and rarely as simple as one might think. The man said that he was having problems with his partner. They had been arguing and there was a lot of negative energy in their home – each blaming the other. He had talked to his doctor but to no avail. The doctor's advice had been to try talking to his partner more – and exercise. There were no helpful drugs for his complaint. The man said that he loved his partner and wanted things to be 'like they use to be'. As he began to open up, he admitted that things were not too good 'in the bedroom' either as they had drifted apart. It had got to the point where he could not 'perform' and, consequently, she felt unloved. Worse still, she accused him of having someone else. Actually he did – his work.

He was obviously distressed and marched up and down amongst the crystals touching and feeling them. It's always interesting to see how, under stress, we adults fight our intuition and resist all of our body's attempts to heal itself. We seem to feel that our intellect has to take control – and dismiss the silly feelings of our emotions. Really we are out of balance but that is a concept that we aren't taught at school and is usually brushed off as being simply out of sorts when we're grown up. Such behaviour usually draws disparaging remarks like 'Must be the wrong time of the month' or 'He must have got out of bed on the wrong side'.

The agitated man and I talked a while about energies and auras. When he was comfortable with these concepts I asked him to consider where he thought the root of the problem lay. Often there are many layers to depression and not everything is exactly what it may seem at first glance. The healer must be aware of this and listen very carefully to both what is being said – and what is not. It would be very irresponsible of me to say something easy like 'Try a piece of Carnelian – that works well with depression', pacify him, make a sale and get him away. One of the most remarkable things about crystals and minerals is that they teach us about ourselves. They help us to face the reality of our being for all its complexities, its positive qualities and its failings. It emerged that, when this man faced the truth, it was the pressure of his work, in trying to meet unattainable deadlines that continually put him under pressure. He was forced to compete with men half his age joining the firm full of new ideas and confidence pouring out of every area of their being. This, and the growing awareness of his own age, was gnawing away at his self-confidence and undermining his sense of security. He was becoming afraid to make that phone call in case of a refusal, frightened to risk new ideas in case of failure in front of the younger men and worrying about meeting target quotas that seemed to increase daily. He was stepping into what, in women, has been unfairly wrapped into 'the menopausal phase' – and he was at a complete loss as to where to find help. Talking about it is half the problem and facing it is the other half. I suggested that he take a piece of Pyrite to place on his desk at work and a few different Tumbled Jaspers to keep in his pocket. I also recommended a smooth Smoky Quartz wand or pyramid and I explained the thinking behind my choice.

The Iron Pyrite was for him to keep on his desk for positiveness. My experience has been that this mineral works on the solar plexus (the 'fight or flight' chakra) and will open this energy centre up for him. It will give him the confidence to make that phone call without thinking about refusal, knowing that if this call is not successful he will make another and another for the law of averages says that one has to be successful – and that's enough. It will help him come to terms with the changing phases in his life and allow him to embrace this change as just another challenge no different from any other. It also works on mental acuity and quick thinking. Diplomacy would aid his popularity amongst his colleagues and, when he no longer sees them as a threat, he won't be putting out negative signals toward them causing tensions at work.

The Tumbled Jaspers were for him to use as worry beads in his pocket. Whenever he felt under stress he would intuitively tumble the stones and, as he did so, they would ground negative energies. Although normally considered a gentle grounding stone, I felt that a few different Jaspers like Brecciated, Unakite and Picture Jasper would calm and control his frustrations.

The smooth Smoky Quartz was for him to use when he had trouble with excess head activity. I felt that it would take away his headaches and work on the brow area, where he held his tensions. To allow him to stop thinking about work and give him an inner understanding, it would penetrate the dark areas in his being and open up the third eye. Using the Smoky Quartz would support his self-esteem and give him the courage to admit to his feelings – balancing his polarities.

The man was happy to take on board what we had discussed and purchased his carefully selected crystals with a willingness to try something new, in spite of his intellectual scepticism. The entire collection cost less then twenty pounds and he was smiling as he left the shop. Many weeks later I had a flying visit from this same man. He thanked me and winked as he told me that things were now working out. I must have the kind of face that people feel they can talk to. I am continually surprised how many men of all ages will actually ask for help and I am comforted that, in this high flying age of success, people are still prepared to look back to basics for answers when things go wrong.

Another example of just talking to people and being receptive was a woman who came to me complaining of sleeping difficulties. My experience has taught me that such problems are seldom cut and dried. Perhaps that is why they seek help from alternative healing therapies. She asked for healing and I gave her spiritual healing. Afterwards she said that she felt as if she had been floating in a beautiful blue bubble and, as it had gently touched the ground, she had stepped out. She had felt completely weightless and could walk without touching the grass beneath her feet. She drifted back to consciousness as I touched her shoulders and she began to cry.

She said she had felt safe while I had been working over her body, and a peace had entered her, allowing her to drift off in the knowledge that she was in safe hands. As she gained a little more control she admitted that she had been having nightmares which had eventually led to her being afraid of going to sleep.

She was afraid of something that she couldn't see. On waking she couldn't remember. I advised her to try going to bed with one piece of White Howlite in one hand and a piece of Blue Howlite in the other. The White Howlite, held in one's hand, calms the pulse until a faint, slow pulse can be felt through the palm. This new pulse is too slow to be your own – and, as you become more aware of it, you feel almost hypnotised into a peaceful dreamy state of total relaxation. The Blue Howlite has a magic of its own that allows you to bring back the wisdom learnt from the dream state or astral travellings. The two crystals together were only a couple of pounds and the woman left feeling much more balanced. It can make a world of difference to someone just being able to sleep peacefully and not afraid to close their eyes. After a week the woman returned. She asked for another healing, which was really her way of asking if we could talk in private. I worked on the healing and felt a lot of head energy moving and swirling around. She had been experiencing an increase in psychic abilities in recent months and that had led to the nightmares. She had no one to talk to about this and thought she was going mad. She said that the pieces of Howlite had helped her to retrieve the pictures and places she visited during her sleep and, of course, the 'known' is never as scary as the 'unknown'. Talking about this had led her to come to terms with the concepts of astral travelling and that she would return back into her body. When one lives and sleeps alone it can be a frightening concept to grasp. Talking to others, who have had similar experiences, helps one to understand they are not alone with this gift and begin to view it as such. She now keeps a diary of her dream walks and sleeps well. Indeed, she now looks forward to sleep with a new anticipation.

No one is going to fool you that the path to enlightenment is easy. If it were, everyone you speak to would be hurrying along the path. In spite of more recent experiments and the explorations into subtle energies, telesomatics etc., science still does not know enough about 'left brain–right brain' activity. We know even less about physical brain–spiritual brain! To me, it makes sense. To become aware we must first learn how to override the physical brain. But, if that is the 'computer' running the functions of the body, there must be a higher source of intelligence communicating instructions. The parts of the brain that we know so little about could therefore logically be 'receiving equipment' – receiving and processing information from our spiritual brain, such as intuition, psychic phenomena etc. The spiritual brain, of course, residing in the 'higher' self – the invisible body of the soul.

I have seen all manner of apparitions around people which, we are led to believe, are departed spirits, angelic beings, monks and even Jesus Christ. I have studied this phenomenon for twenty years or more and, though I am fully prepared to change my point of view in the light of more information, I have drawn my own conclusions. When I work as a medium, reading the 'auric beans', I can pick up a lot of information about the subject in front of me. Usually, this begins with how they are feeling physically and emotionally as I begin to 'attune'. But as I am given more to see, I start to feel, and sometimes see, forms around them. What fascinates me most about this phenomenon is that, depending on one's state of comprehension and level of awareness, people seem to carry around with them exactly what they expect to be there. For example, if they are a follower of the Christian faith and consider themselves to be truly religious, the information channelled for them comes in the form of facets of Jesus. He will stand beside them and show the way. If they are a Buddhist I will often see, standing beside them, a Buddhist monk – and so on for shamanism and many other religions. Another person commonly seen is a mother, grandmother or father figure, etc. These apparitions will give encouragement, bring love and even help us by conveying messages as clues to the predictable outcome of events in our life. This information is valued because of who it comes from – someone they trust. The message might mean nothing to them if it came from their higher self as they do not believe in themselves. Because of this I believe destiny is not written – but that our higher selves can see the bigger picture and aid our journey. It cannot, however, make the journey for us. If the only way through is to camouflage the medicine then that is how it is done.

I have a friend, also a medium, and we have spent time together in the past performing a number of experiments, studying and trying to understand what happens on the 'other side'. We had studied together, in 'circle' and 'rescue' work, by following newly-departed spirits over to the other side, trying to see where they went and with whom. On one such journey we were astounded to find out that a recently departed acquaintance of my friend's was seated in what we had come to know as the 'Halls of Learning', talking to three beings of light. They were radiant in appearance and obviously in deep conversation. When we discussed this later, my friend asked what I had seen and I told her. She said that she had seen the same thing – but found it unbelievable that her departed friend would sit talking to such beings. He had, apparently, never been the 'spiritual type' and did not believe in an after life. Unless death itself had brought about some great intellectual trans-formation, this was very out of character. So what she had done whilst he was talking was to position herself behind him and look through his eyes to see what he could see. Sure enough he was seeing three elderly monks in long habits with whom he was perfectly comfortable. My friend and I had seen three beings of light – so what were they really?

More and more reports of such events are coming forward as we reach the start of the new millennium. I don't think that these phenomena are becoming any more frequent. I think that we are simply becoming more comfortable talking about them. Science, particularly medicine, has finally stopped 'laughing' at some of the claims made by healers and metaphysicians, now turning some serious attention to empirical studies of the most fundamental concepts in question. The Space Agency NASA has funded research into the energies of crystals and minerals for the past fifteen years. The Bioenergetics Laboratory, part of the Life Sciences Department of NASA's Goddard Flight Centre, conducts experiments into the nature and properties of crystal and mineral energies – and their effects on the human energy fields. 'Distance diagnosis' has been the subject of some serious studies in the USA. Perhaps the most notable would be those conducted by neurosurgeon Norman Shealy and published in his book *The Creation of Health*. In a controlled series of experiments, with clairvoyant diagnostician Carolyn Myss, he reports a success rate of 93%. The scientific study of these new subtle energies has even given birth to a new terminology. The area of telesomatics is attracting more and more attention. Telesomatics is the ability to effect physical or physiological change on another – by thought. William Braud and Marilyn Schlitz of the Mind Science Foundation in San Antonio, Texas, have conducted hundreds of controlled experiments to test the impact of mental imagery – sent from a healer – on the physiology of the 'receiver'. These recipients were both distant (sometimes over a thousand miles away) and unaware that such imagery was being sent to them. Their experiments brought them to two conclusions. The first is that such 'thought transmissions' were able to produce very noticeable change in the recipient's physiology – and the second is that the individual was able to produce even more distinctive changes on their physiology *through their own mental imagery*. In cases where the two techniques were combined (i.e. both healer and recipient sharing the same imagery) the results showed an 80% measurable improvement in the recipient's health.

Healers have long known of this power that seems to lie within all of us – needing only to be encouraged through time and practice. Cultures as far apart as Africa and America have been using these gifts for millennia. The African witch doctor draws his power from the belief of the villagers, making them willing recipients of his telesomatic influences. Our friends amongst the native American elders have given us many examples of telesomatic healings over the years. Even the noted explorer Sir James Frazer, in his study of the rituals of native Americans, *The Golden Bough*, describes sand-painting rituals, katchina dances and many other examples of healing methods from over a century ago. Those of you who, reading this, still harbour doubts about the power of the mind – I would ask that you simply try it yourself. The mind is the most powerful component in our existence. And it is that part of us nearest to the cosmos. Little wonder that science still understands so little of it.

Ten negative steps to disease.

1   **Attack on the system.** Any aggressive physical attack or emotional attack will cause a noticeable reaction. The response is that the weakest energy centre on the physical body reacts by spinning erratically. This action has a reaction on the other centres as they try to regain a balance. It can be possible from just one severe attack to suddenly create an imbalance powerful enough to push all the necessary 'buttons' to induce self-destruction. Most people throughout their lives encounter a little disturbance

now and then and quickly learn to readjust. There are times, however, when one is more vulnerable. When one negative effect suddenly escalates and becomes many – causing an 'inward-spiral' effect.

2 **Negative attitude.** Behaviour patterns can sometimes become self-destructive. Guilt can rear it's ugly head, when one tries hard to address a situation, followed by blame when one seeks to quantify and excuse it – especially when it involves someone we love. Denial is also a key player when we try to pretend that incidents never happened in order to keep the peace. All these behaviours simply push the problem deeper into the psyche where it will gnaw away at our foundations.

3 **Lack of rest.** When our sleeping pattern and relaxation times are disturbed, we quickly feel unsettled and our concentration deteriorates through worry.

4 **Emotional deterioration.** Exhaustion, resulting from constant tiredness, and being cut-off from our spiritual connection to source leads inevitably to feelings of unworthiness and low self-esteem. We become ashamed to confide or talk about the problem.

5 **Inactivity.** The exhaustion results in a lack of exercise and movement in the chakras slows down. The emotional decline and exhaustion worsens.

6 **Depression.** The constant worry and depression lead to an unhealthy excess of 'head activity' worsened by the feelings of hopelessness and melancholy.

7 **Anxiety.** Fear and strain now create tension which appears to lower the immune system. This has a knock-on effect, leading to a low or poor appetite and irregular eating patterns. Smoking, drinking or pills often become a crutch to periodically relieve the depression. This adds extra elements for an already distressed system to cope with. The

natural defence system of the body is now trying hard to communicate and reconnect to source for a charge of positive energy. Drinking, smoking and drugs act as blocks. They stop the body's natural abilities to heal by confusing the signals. The body is distressed, depressed and out of balance. It needs to be reconnected to the spiritual body as soon as possible. However advice from friends like 'Cheer yourself up and have a drink' only adds more to the confusion of an already overloaded system. The emotional body readjusts to the intake of chemicals receiving false signals. Then, as the effects wear off, the body has to try to adjust itself yet again. By this time both the physical and emotional bodies are exhausted from this merry-go-round and continue on a downward spiral.

8 **Pressure.** This is a critical point and, at this moment, the health can go either way. If there is an outlet for the frustrations, someone to talk to who cares or something worthwhile to believe in, there is still a great deal of hope. If neither can be found the negative cycle gathers momentum. Pressure from colleagues and friends to be less depressing to be around results in putting on an act, which in turn leads to more suppression. Because the effort can become immense, the crutches required to sustain the façade need to be increased. At this stage the aura reacts by shrinking around the body. As the energy reduces so does the strength of the aura. It compacts around the body to protect itself and let nothing in. Unfortunately, that includes the connection to source. The density of the aura is heavy around the physical body and in turn weighs one down. The picture seen by the outside world is one of an introverted and troubled person.

9 **Detachment and separation.** The vibrations have now been lowered significantly and the energy output reduced.

The lower the vibration of the physical body the harder it is for it to communicate through its spiritual or emotional body. The signal is weak and unclear so little or no sustenance can be received from the divine energy.

10 **Disease.** This will always affect the weakest genetic disposition. It is the body's natural alarm system that something is drastically wrong and the body needs immediate rebalancing in order to survive. Illness is the physical manifestation of the cause.

Ten positive steps toward healing with crystals

10 **Natural instinct.** We feel ourselves drawn toward a certain crystal or mineral.

9 **Identification.** Like comparative energy attracted to like, one is receptive to the other – reflecting that need in each. Once that link has been established, the 'I'm not so alone' force has prised open a small crack within the dense auric field. Instantly, this will allow a minute amount of the distress signal to escape and, the 'desire to be healed' vibration to transmit a positive, identifiable current.

8 **Reduced pressure.** Crystals do not put one under any pressure or ask anything in return. There is no timescale for improvement and their only function at this point is to stabilise the body's condition. The two comparative energies balance each other and quickly reach an equilibrium.

7 **Normal diet resumes.** A more healthy diet resumes naturally when pressure is reduced. It is at this stage that many will start to laugh at themselves as the illogicality of

their predicament hits home. 'Acquire a crystal and heal your life'. However, even that thought pattern sends out a signal through the aura of being less 'up-tight' and the aura expands as the vibration is raised. Through the laughter the small crack in the aura becomes a little bigger and more energy feeds the aura. The vibration is lifted and, at this point, the body is often naturally attracted to a different crystal. Many find themselves asking 'Why was I ever attracted to such an ordinary crystal before when there are so many beautiful ones I never even noticed'. Well the answer is because that was how they felt. Unnoticed and unloved. Now they feel a shift to a higher vibration and so require a crystal that reflects it.

6   **Strengthened immunity.** The link to source is now established and so starts to feed the spirit which, in turn, feeds the emotional body – which feeds the physical body.

5   **The depression lifts.** Things no longer seem so hopeless and positive steps are being taken to reverse the negative attack on the system. One's 'crutches' are needed less and less as confidence returns. Drugs are reduced, smoking and comfort foods reduce allowing the body to naturally detoxify.

4   **Energy increases.** The body naturally has more energy due to the increase of food intake. The metabolic rate speeds up and one feels noticeably more 'alive'.

3   **Relaxation and sleep resume.** The extra energy output guarantees a good night's rest. Energy levels continue to rise, resulting in a better overall balance within the system.

2   **Positive attitude returns.** Behaviour patterns become self-promoting and the personality takes on the responsibility of aiding the system. The crystals at this point can work on all the energy centres. A total re-balancing is taking place.

The attitude improves day by day and the physical body begins to return to normal.

1   **Health is restored.** Vitality and wholeness. The ability to think and process information correctly works on the stress-related anxieties. Confidence, patience and self-control are all restored. The body is connected to source and functioning at its best ability. The crystals become 'old friends' and have suddenly found a place within you. They become our teachers and, because they are usually accessible, are always around.

Once one has come to terms with a serious disease or illness the mind often struggles with concepts like purpose. 'If everything is for a reason and coincidences do not exist, what is the message or lesson I am supposed to learn from it'. It is one of those questions that can and does change peoples' lives and is happening all the time. One answer, from the native American elders I have spoken with, is quite simply this. 'When we forget who we are the Great Spirit has ways of reminding his children not only who they are but what it is they promised to return and do. We are all part of the Great Mystery and no single warrior has more to do then he is capable of. Some have more to do than others and that is their choice. There is no purpose in one remembering all. In the physical world of matter it becomes a burden to him. He will be reminded when the time comes. When we stray too far away from our chosen path, in order to be separated and individual, we create disease and our lesson is to learn to find our way back.'

When asked for a general list of ailments and suggested crystals to treat them I find it hard to pinpoint exactly which would be the all round best choice. For all the reasons described before, it is never quite that simple. Some say there is a Calcite for every chakra and, as a safe bet, I can assure you there is. They come in as many colours as the chakras. Figure 1 shows a diagram of the location of the chakras and the crystals I have found to be most successful in dealing with imbalances.

This is my own way of explaining it to my children not too far removed from the way the native American story tellers explain it to their children. Perhaps in its simplicity it allows us to get our heads around something – of which there is no real explanation other then it just 'is'.

Your evolution began long before you could even speak. When you were a mere sparkle of energy that hurled it's way through the cosmos. As momentum gathered, the energy built until it eventually cracked like thunder. Your first transformation had now taken place – you now were negative and positive. Matter entered your being. As energy and matter, you were an uncut diamond, rough, but in equality containing both 'god and goddess' energies. As mineral and crystal tumbled through time and space, you recorded information, like a library. You were taught patience deep within the womb of the great Earth Mother. Evolution is slow and gradual, and your being is dense and heavy. Change comes as you equate the different vibrations felt by the evolution of the Mother herself. Times of incredible heat followed by times of unbelievable cold. Without eyes in the darkness your senses come into being. Eventually, lovingly nurtured toward your next transformation, the Earth Mother gives you birth and expels you from her womb. Now, ground down like fine sand, you've entered the nursery. Here you experience growth, pushing down your roots for nourishment and lifting your head to seek enlightenment. You learn of the elements, the seasons, the Sun and the Moon, for you have entered the world of the trees and the plants.

When you are in balance you are like the strong sturdy branches and trunk of a cedar or oak. You are home to all types of insect and beings from the emerging animal kingdom – your brothers. Your leaves give beauty and shade. A pleasure for those who stand and watch the dancing of the wind spirits. Your roots go deep and nourish the physical body. They 'ground' you and keep you upright. They connect you to the Earth Mother and remind you from whence you came. Trees give oxygen to purify the air, and fruit and leaves to sustain life. From trees we learn about the seasons, accepting change as a natural cycle of regeneration. Not all trees are big and strong and your time spent in the tree world teaches you many valuable lessons. Even the mighty oak loses its leaves and dies back in winter. This teaches the importance of rest and rejuvenation. A time of action and a time to withdraw and store energy. Some trees are old and wise whilst some are young and foolish. Some bend in the wind and sway in the breeze whilst others stand rigid and straight. Your journey through the plant and tree kingdom teach you above all to always grow toward the light.

The cycle over, you decompose. Returning to the ground and, washed down into the streams – the very veins of the Earth, your journey continues into the waters of the ocean where, through the passage of time, you enjoy your first taste of life. Tentative steps out into the unknown without the warmth of the Earth Mother's womb to protect you. Here in the playgrounds of the waters you learn about emotions. Feelings of joy, the freedom to be splashed about and taken where the tides and winds should desire, or feelings of sadness and anger as darkness encroaches to spoil the fun. Tears are like your emotions, they cannot be held and are a natural release of tensions that flow from your being. In the waters you learn about the magnetism of the magical Moon and her moods – and soon realise that she makes a powerful ally.

Having graduated, you next crawl onto the land to take your place as a beast of the Earth. Each time you return you learn new strengths of intuition and cunning. Instincts and impulses, along with survival, heighten your sense of awareness. Eventually you are ready to fly and take to the sky. From this vantage point you can obtain a higher perspective. You practise rising and falling at incredible speeds. Hovering and being tossed on the breezes and rising currents, you experience the air. Air is light and expanding, difficult to measure and contain. It represents the world of thought. The ability of reason comes with thought and, when learnt, raises you above the clouds. It heightens your perception of pain and pleasure to carry you on with direction.

At last, the driving force of the universe is behind you and you are man. Thinking, feeling, walking, talking. A real live 'humane' being. Science searches for understanding of evolution. I believe it will never find what it seeks on the physical plane because it is not physical. The evolution of man is in the invisible dimension of the soul. When we remember the 'art of remembering' we will each have our own record of our journey. Each will vary, depending how quickly we learnt and how many mistakes we made.

Rocks teach one the gifts of patience and sight and, like a computer, one learnt to be a record keeper. To sit around for thousands of years observing the universe is a very good lesson. The body of the Earth Mother is made of matter. She is like all things that breathe and live – just of a denser quality. To remember to 'see with the eyes of a rock' means to use a supreme method of vision. From out of the density of matter energy must be channelled to emanate and see without eyes. Rocks are the energy keepers, they teach the ability to see clearly through all our physical illusions.

Life in the plant kingdom taught us about roots and taking time to reconnect to the Earth Mother. They teach us about giving and healing. In all plants lie hidden properties. Some teach us lessons like the rowan tree that teaches us about protection. The grand old oaks teach us about strength of character and healing of the spine. To remember life in the plant kingdom is a great knowledge that would fill volumes and yet each of us has that potential.

Freedom in the waters was a great breakthrough. We learnt of emotions as strong as the tides and swam in the blood of the Earth Mother, just as if she had given us birth from the streams into the mighty oceans. To experience feelings of both our male and female. We will always remember that water is life. Water can be as solid as ice – hard, stubborn and unmoving. It can also be warm and fluid. It can rise high as a huge wave or sink deep down to the very depths of the ocean bed. It can be pleasure and pain, sometimes in the same moment. To know and have experienced the element of water is to have lived emotion.

The animal kingdom alerted new senses. You are only as powerful as your powers of perception and therefore must remember to stay awake! To receive, collate and act on the information of your senses. Your hearing and sense of smell became vital to survival. The animal instinct is always just under the surface and should never be dismissed. It warns of predators, deceit and dangers long before they raise there ugly head, and recognises 'soul mates' instantly.

The lessons acquired once evolved into the bird kingdom taught us much about dealing with flight. To prepare one to travel on air, to soar and return. The spaciousness of the sky, the warmth of the sun. The light and the breadth of vision that carries us along – as long as we keep sight of our truth. Air teaches thought and with thought comes reason. To circle high like an eagle and use this vantage point to see all that blocks your path to freedom is to remember your evolution through the manifestations of the winged realms.

The many transformations that make man are all necessary. The lessons learnt require a complete understanding before progression onto the next stage. The comprehension and responsibility of guardians of the Earth Mother. Man, Her child, fails Her relentlessly yet, like a true Mother, She allows him freedom to grow. However, when he oversteps the mark and begins a path that will do damage to Herself or himself, She will intervene. All that man requires to complete the transition into the spiritual realms is available to him. His path is all around him as a constant reminder of who he is and where he has been. In the meantime, as guardian, he requires the knowledge to keep himself in balance. Crystals and minerals hold that memory. They trigger the vital cord that allows us to communicate with our higher self. Our 'true' being that recalls everything about the evolution of our soul. It acts by flicking a switch in our psychic awareness that transcends time and space. By just allowing that natural feeling to lead you will instinctively choose the correct crystal or mineral for you. It may not be the same one each time, for as one blockage is cleared another may need adjusting. However, with patience, rocks and minerals teach us much about ourselves. They help us compose a picture that makes up the blueprint of the soul. Treating the symptoms in isolation does nothing to restore the balance of the vital life force that drives the body. The life force has its own connection to source which draws the energy needed to generate the body's own capacity to protect, balance, regenerate and heal itself physically, mentally, emotionally and spiritually.

2

The
human
aura

The human beanbag

There is much written about the human energy field with many interpretations of the aura's appearance and what is considered healthy or otherwise. Many cultures have made reference to the aura in one form or another. In fact I feel quite sure that Joseph's 'Coat of many colours', referred to in the Old Testament, was actually his aura. It is a subject that has interested academics for

centuries and one that still continues to elude scientific understanding. Even with new and advanced technology there is still,
for example, no camera to date that can reliably capture the
human aura – in spite of being able to photograph other forms
of the human energy field.

We are dealing with an 'unknowable', as our native elders
constantly remind us. How and why some people and not
others are able to see the aura may best be explained in this way.
The physical body is a very complicated, finely tuned piece of
equipment of which many functions are still not adequately
understood. Vision is one such area. For example, our eyes
actually view everything upside down. It is the brain that turns
the picture over for us to relate to. Our eyes are extremely
sensitive and, I believe, can also see the energy that exists
around everything. However, it would be very difficult to
function 'normally' with vivid luminous colours attached and
pulsating around everything. There are certain functions which
are 'reticular' – like breathing, sweating and shivering etc. Then
there are the 'anticipated' functions that the brain overrides and
takes care of – like walking up stairs. Once we have learnt to
walk and balance, then negotiated a few obstacles, walking
upstairs becomes easy. We do not have to program ourselves
each time we encounter a staircase. Likewise, I believe, part of
the brain adjusts our visual perception allowing objects of
matter to become more clearly focused fields of energy. It could
be a case of the brain deciding what we need to know and what
we don't. The question I would most like answered is this. Did
man ever have the ability to see auras and energy as part of his
'hunter-animal' instinct – and then evolve to a point where he
no longer required this function? Did the brain override our
ability to use the faculty or – are we only now evolving to
the point where we can relate to, and understand, the energy –
matter equation, thus heightening our visual perception.

I have always been able to see and feel energy around people, animals and plants and have been aware of energy within crystals for many years. I have never ceased to be amazed at the variations in the luminous colours of these emanations. I never stop questioning this faculty and, as I have grown spiritually, I have become more aware how much power we have over words, intentions and deeds – and the effects we cause with them. Indeed, it places on us a great responsibility for every thought or action. A number of years ago, these thoughts inspired me to write a short verse that expressed the feelings and thoughts that this ability was showing me . . . It's called:

Colours of life

As pure as the whitest carpet of snow,
The palest of pastels only innocence knows,
Nurtured into colours red, yellow, blue – bright,
Primary basics so often delight

Like splashes of colour we laugh through schooldays
Big rainy puddles splashed all different ways,
Loud, bold extremes in face-finger painting
With no inhibitions to stop us creating

Then 'teenage' years, as so often prove,
that independence changes the colours of youth,
Dark, violent purples, symbolic relations
Changing the world, new generations

The 'in between' years so quickly fly
Earning a living – just getting by,
Colours more muted, confused always tired
Reflect in the actions and pace one acquired

Raw umbers, yellow ochres and earth-colours smoulder
Relaxed by the fire, old head on old shoulders,
Accepting each day as a 'God-given' gift
The wisdom of age – only learned when one's lived.

With practice and patience it is possible to close certain faculties down, like feeling and sensing auras, to allow our mind to concentrate on others things. Our physical, everyday functions and family life for example. Very often it is only times when I am out and about, and my concentration wanders, that I suddenly become aware of the intensity of other people's auras all around me. Then I find my attention is drawn to the erratic or unusual ones. The ill or overexcited, extrovert or introverted characters who make up the contrasts of life.

I have never read a book that describes auras in the way I see them or relates to them as I do for diagnosis. So I have reached the conclusion that what is considered right for one person may not be correct for another. I hope this will help many people who doubt their abilities as healers or mediums because their way of seeing or working does not conform. Here, at last, I will try to explain in simple terms how a human aura appears to me.

Picture a beanbag in the shape of a human being. Now try to visualise broad bands of luminous colour expanding upwards from the feet and through to the crown of the head. Imagine most of the colours slightly denser than rainbow colours except for the feet and legs. In what I consider to be healthy people the feet and legs are usually more earthy colours of gold, rust and ochre. This, I assume, is due to being connected to the Earth and walking in balance. The top of the legs bring orange bands then red, orange again, yellow, lime green, leaf green, blue, purple and usually, at the very top of the crown, gold or white light. Arms are normally the lime green of the centre just below the heart and because people generally move there arms about when they talk I find that it is this colour and part of the body that draws my attention first.

In the centre of the body, vertically along the spinal column, the 'beans' become not only more dense in colour but also appear to form into vortices, spirals of energy, and each colour seems to have its own vortex. We have come to know these centres as chakras and they are apparent in many teachings. The beans that make up the rest or the majority of the body emanate energy at a vibration that depend on the body's state of being.

Auras

Auras are the 'invisible' beans that surround the physical body and are felt by most people as their intuition starts working. They are tinged by the colour of the corresponding energy centre and the appearance is somewhat like liquid soap bubbles. Draped around the body as living and moving energy, they form a sort of haze and it is this that you tune into if you walk into a room full of people. As like attracts like there are always those you feel comfortable with and those you simply don't.

When you meet someone for the first time it is considered unacceptable to prejudge them just by a feeling, but that is actually exactly what most of us do. A feeling is an emotion, an emotion is energy, it is all very basic. It is intuition, but not as quantifiable as the senses of smell or vision. Our eyes play a huge part in as much as we assimilate things like colour, race, age, sex – not to mention beauty and dress. Our nose decides whether we can tolerate the odour surrounding someone, perfumes, deodorants, cigarettes etc., but also the underlying natural scent of the body. However, what plays a much more fundamental role is the aura. It tells us what the energy of that person is really like and is picked up by a whole array of our senses and not simply our eyes. There's a lot of truth the saying 'Beauty is just skin deep'.

The colour beans that make up the body are like atoms of matter containing energy and therefore more dense than the aura itself. The aura is made up of energy containing the 'memory of matter' with just as many beans, if not more, but these are, to all intent and purpose, invisible. It is possible to see this energy field around someone either naturally or by lifting your vibration. I have noticed that at times of stress when the metabolic rate is racing, the pineal gland in the crown chakra is responsible for the release of melatonin, which sedates the brain. This overriding of basic physical functions seems to lift the vibration and the auric energy field is more easily visible. Some refer to this as the 'veils of enlightenment' being gradually lifted. The ideal state would be that of meditation to reach this level of awareness.

Children are more likely to see auras naturally and, providing this faculty is not suppressed, they retain the gift through adolescence. I have also found that many adults who see auras have discovered this gift after some traumatic experience, that has heightened their sensitivity, or through an illness slowing them down and offering them with an opportunity to question and think.

As the beans around the body spin out they become more dissipated and form strings, like pearls, that find connections within all things. For example, they stretch out and connect to distant trees and plants. This, amongst other things, can provide much needed grounding. They touch minerals and crystals that, in turn, can recognise energy centres requiring attention. They interact with animals identifying traits in one's nature and personality. They also drift in and out of other people's auras and feed off of their energy or, alternatively, feed them. This is commonly known as a 'psychic vampire' attack and, if not controlled, can lead to a depletion of one's energy – especially in someone who is not connected to the great 'generator' in the universe. People who work with the elderly or in hospitals etc., are all susceptible to this form of vampirism and can become quite ill themselves unless they are able to disconnect from it all. Those who wish to work in these fields, but are extremely sensitive, need to be aware not only of this phenomenon but also of how to deal with it.

The paradox is that although we are physically separate in matter from all things we are also connected to all things – by energy. Every person living or dead who ever existed contains a facet of being that each and every one of us is capable of achieving, be it negative or positive. Through the strands of the aura that reach out in every direction we are all connected. The difference is in the fine tuning of our receiving equipment. We all are capable of channelling directly from source and utilising that energy. The very thing that blocks most of us – is ourselves. We are conditioned to believing that we need permission from some 'higher being' rather than take responsibility for our own actions and the universal laws of cause and effect.

Out in bright sunshine or in brightly lit places the vibrance of some people's aura can blind me and I find myself stepping back and shading my eyes. Sometimes I find myself drawn to an aura on the other side of a restaurant or in some public place and have to exert great discipline not to stare too obviously. When we are being observed we know it intuitively and normally eye contact is made. This first encounter is an important exchange of energy. Either it is sexual, which is a fast vibration, a loving emotional glance, which is a mutual calm balanced vibration, or an unnerving feeling of being watched. This incurs a slow, intrusive and cool vibration that can quickly surround and chill your very being. Depending on the vibration picked up, one instinctively knows from where and why someone is staring at them. There are many reasons one person catches your eye, but each is an exchange of energy and, if you are relaxed and your guard is down, your aura is open and accessible – making it easily penetrable by others. This, of course, could also place you in a vulnerable position. Later I shall go into more depth about protection but, for now, it is enough to say each of us has the ability to shield ourselves under such circumstances. Figure 2 shows the 'appearance' of a normal, healthy aura.

The body's first line of defence

Although no one likes to feel pain, it is necessary. It is the body's way of attracting immediate attention and, without it, a cut or burn could often prove even more damaging. However, in circumstances where attention to an open wound is not the answer and yet the body is struggling to retain balance, symptoms will often manifest in the form of illness. It is the body's way of bringing one's attention to the cause of stress in one's life and, if given a chance, the opportunity to heal itself. The problem is that, in most cases, we expect far too much from the body with very little or no maintenance. We hurtle through life with high expectations of the equipment we have been given and are totally surprised when something goes wrong. In fact we really just want to go to a doctor for them to 'fix' the problem and send us on our way. We do not want to take responsibility for our health or deal with the cause. A few pills or a replacement part is much more convenient.

Looking for the root cause of an illness can, in many cases, mean change. Unfortunately many of us become complacent and resist change, clinging to what we know and feel comfortable with even if it is not good or healthy for us. Change, even for the better, can be a scary prospect and, as a problem is never solved on the same level as it manifests, it usually involves changing the way we think – which is never easy. Addressing these issues will not only aid, if not eradicate, the health problem, it will also shift one's awareness and, perhaps, the direction of one's life. Some say that we each have a guardian angel who is responsible for making sure that we achieve all we set out to in our lifetime. Their duty is to nudge us along if we should wander too far away from our path. A telephone call would be nice but then again it goes back to the quality of our receiving equipment.

Illness manifesting in the aura

What can the energy surrounding the body tell us? Well the first thing is the movement of the energy waves themselves. Whether they are calm, grounded, excitable, erratic, wobbly, enveloping, broken or disconnected. The next thing is the size and projected distance of the energy. This can vary considerably from a few inches to several metres. Lastly is the colour – and opinions differ on this perhaps more than anything else but it would be true to say that what you 'see' and 'relate to' would be correct for you. Most of the time, I feel and sense energy in the same way as most healers. It is only when I doubt myself that my higher self seems to decide to show me the aura in colour to aid my diagnosis. It is for this reason that I have studied the auric body so intensely and have reached the conclusion that it has little to do with the eyes and more to do with perception.

For anyone who has never seen an aura I can help by telling you it looks like heat rising in the distance from a tarmac road on a hot day. Add the sun shining through a rainbow for colours and it pretty much sums up an aura. Blue, green and yellow are most commonly seen along with red in young adults and orange in children. Purple is only usual in advanced souls or intensely spiritual people. It is calm, sensitive, understanding, kind and healing. Earthy colours are stable grounded people, reliable and honest. White or golden light surrounds truth and innocence. Strands of this are often seen around the elderly or dying. It seems to be a transitional stage, where the physical body is moving into the auric body. Dark brown or black hanging heavy in the aura is something that, thankfully, I have only seen twice. They were around very malevolent beings – totally devoid of compassion. Needless to say these colours will always get my attention. Vibrant lime green is often seen around the heart and arms and, for me, indicates enthusiasm and energy. These people have a passion for all they do – be it artistic, creative, self-sacrificing. They are people full of love. In adults, yellow–orange in the body area makes me weary. It emanates anxiety, jealousy and pus. It shows me impatience, haste and not enough attention to detail. Blue is self-control, patience, peace, tran-quillity. Found around people who are prepared to work at or through something in their own way and time. They are good to be around – a positive influence to others. Red is the sexual base colour and, when seen, can mean haste, impatience, materialism and drive. It's great for getting things done but it can be like living in a whirlwind and requires an opposite to ground and channel it.

Some auras have beans of colour shooting out of certain chakras, like fountains or plumes, coming straight from the universal spirit and shifting energy out through the mouths or hands – like those of healers. Some auras seem to bulge out of areas around the body. This would indicate that there is an imbalance. It is one of the first signs of illness. Likewise, an area where the energy appears to be leaking and flowing out as if it's been punctured. This auric energy 'spill' can be caused by a number of issues but, if it's not corrected, it will certainly result in the person becoming ill or depressed. Depression is often the strange underlying factor in many illnesses and can be seen in the aura. First as dull patches becoming grey and eventually as gaping holes. All this is usually going on while the person is maintaining the 'I'm fine – everything is wonderful' impression to the outside world and trying hard to convince themselves. They delude themselves with thoughts like 'Ignore it and it does not exist' or 'I don't want to change anything in my life so I shall pay no attention to it – and it will go away'.

This is the time healing probably works at its best. If only healing were to be sought at this stage, just by balancing the aura and introducing a little calm into the mixture, a bigger picture may be viewed. Life can become a runaway train and, by stepping back and seeing the potential outcome, we could find a more positive direction and save a lot of energy. Unfortunately, because at this stage little or no symptoms are felt other than frustration or agitation, little is usually done. After all, who takes the time to teach us the warning signs?

Stress or agitation shown in the aura

When people complain of being in a state of complete agitation and unable to think clearly, it can often be a number of issues that cause the condition. Firstly, the metabolism can be racing through stress, exertion or excitement for example. Next, take a note of the clothes worn by the person. Are they natural fibres or synthetic? Check the footwear. A lot of static energy can build up on the human body and it needs to be grounded. The type of clothes we wear can have an effect. Our environment is also important. Living and working indoors all the time gives us less chance to feel connected and grounded. People suffering a lot of agitation should aim to spend a short time out in the open air every day. The food we eat and the times at which we eat can play a major role in our balance. 'Little and often' is far better then one mega-meal before bedtime. A variety of foods is much better then sticking to a favoured few fast ready meals. Part of the ritual of paying respect to the body as a temple is in the acquiring and preparing of the food that will sustain the body. Dare I say – 'we are what we eat'.

If the metabolic rate is racing the energy output can be immense and I have measured this on a multimeter. The beans send out a current of electricity similar to a static charge. I have felt and observed that, depending on the material in the clothing and footwear of the person, a charge can build until eventually a complete sense of agitation induces a migraine type headache. This becomes apparent by a fuzzy movement in the beans accumulating in the head area and the beans becoming denser and heavier (see Figure 2). I have also noted that it is possible to relieve a lot of the pressure by getting the person to hold the cold water tap to ground the static.

Shock or violence shown in the aura

In the case of a severe shock the aura tightens around the body, as if trying to close down the emotional body and protect from further trauma. The beans become darker and more compact within the body. The beans in the aura become almost still and without energy. Shock hits the body first in the solar plexus energy centre like an impact which sends the beans spinning outward just as if one were to hit a beanbag. A 'dent' appears and all the beans move out, leaving a crater in the middle. This reaction is followed by the body having trouble with the breathing. It can usually manage only shallow breathing with occasional gulps of deep breath. This largely cuts off the connection to source and, therefore, the body's ability to restore or repair quickly the damage caused. The longer this 'out of balance' state exists the greater the damage to the body. The scenario applies to physical violence. No matter what part of the body is attacked, the effect on the solar plexus is the same (see Figure 4).

The importance of the solar plexus in healing

The solar plexus is a very important chakra in as much as it mediates between the higher and lower chakras. Our ancestors had a variety of legends, myths and stories that explained many of these concepts. Although mostly allegorical, I find these stories are often powerful visualising aids, helping us to clearly understand interrelationships that are otherwise elusive. I tend to use them liberally when I'm trying to explain some of these concepts. Perhaps there is an enormous guardian who lives in the solar plexus, protecting the mighty and magical 'tree of life' positioned within this centre, and, once the secrets of the centre are revealed to you, you will have passed through the Garden of Eden and innocence is yours no more. It houses the intuitive emotions – fear, love, grief, envy, pride etc. Unlike the base chakra, for example, which houses drive, desire, ambition and our taste for adventure and experience. These are derived from the sex centre or kundalini energy.

The solar plexus needs to be activated by a person's consciousness and awareness but, once activated, it is a powerful ally. It is awakened by the heart centre, working through the ethereal bodies with emotional energy. It needs the drive and desire of the kundalini energy centre to push it through and awaken the sensitivity needed to receive the etheric vibrations but, once achieved, its resilience gathers to protect against encroachment from the lower etheric plains. It is for this reason that the kundalini energy must not be awakened before it is ready. The centres do not flow from bottom to top, so to push them up from the base centre could be quite dangerous. There is a definite order to the energy centres of the physical body which relates to the etheric body. It is possible to burn through the silver threads that protect each centre, causing a lot of damage. These silver threads are known to some as veils and others know them as webs. They connect the physical and spiritual centres.

In the chapter on configurations I will go into the correct awakening of the kundalini energy more thoroughly. I have spent much time and effort working to understand this energy centre and have had difficulty trying to express in words something so simple and natural, yet so complex. This is the centre of awareness where the physical and spiritual come together and where they also separate. It is where the energy 'emotion' resides during one's lifetime – and can prove to be the hardest quest and greatest stumbling block. The ability to truly love is to melt into another in totality. To understand this concept is asking one to take every barrier down and leave oneself totally unprotected. This very act, if reciprocated however, can mean balance between the male and female energies – nurturing each to a point of perfection. No ego. Dissect and pull each apart and you would not find that love within them. It resides in the soul and spirit of each so that, in the physical, it can never be found. This is the feeling, the emotional magnetism that cannot be put into words – there simply are no words for it. It happens in the etheric spheres where no words are spoken The solar plexus receives the signal as an emotion which turns the wheel in the base chakra causing the kundalini to rise, releasing hormones and creating the physical attraction. In summary, sex is the physical response whereas love is the etheric response.

I hope this all makes sense because now I need to take this concept a stage further. As we progress in our awareness, the reality dawns of each being on their own path. For a while we may walk along parallel paths and share ideas but ultimately we must each find our own way. It is great to support each other and 'prop' one another up when one stumbles. It is ideal to find a soul mate, but even that does not make one complete. Let me take you back to the male and female energies being in balance, only this time within you. We each have another side and it can take great courage to face our 'other self'. The dark side of one's nature – the side we keep in the shadows – can prove extremely useful. Knowing one's limits or one's power. Whether we talk of male and female or negative and positive we have to truly know ourselves. We have to accept and love ourselves for what we are before we can consciously draw in enough energy to turn the wheels of the chakras and utilise their energy. Done correctly, we do not burn out the webs between the chakras before they are ready. Instead, they begin to dissolve as our awareness grows. If we have the capability of immense anger it can be viewed as a negative aspect, but when used and channelled for positive good it can be extremely useful. That is the difference between a good healer and a *very* good healer – knowing one's equipment.

The solar plexus centre gets its name from the solar energy of our Sun and draws its energy from it. Our spirit comes into the physical through the solar plexus and our spirit leaves from this same centre. Many cultures talk of a gold or silver thread that connects our astral or etheric body via our solar plexus to our physical body during spirit travelling and dream walking. It is this same thread that eventually shrivels and separates on our death. An interesting concept I have come to rely on is that man is both physical and etheric when he walks on the Earth, but on his death he leaves his physical body behind to nourish the Earth Mother whilst his etheric body is free to travel. In the physical world of matter, man experiences and grows, but it is the invisible body that feeds him and sustains him on his path.

This connection through the solar plexus can be explained by thinking of each chakra as a wheel – a medicine wheel. When we breathe, the wheel of the solar plexus turns. If we breathe deeply it turns freely. If we breathe shallowly we do not draw in the full potential of life force. Thus the potential of our vibration is reduced. This role of the solar plexus is most important. The ability to draw in life force and utilise it is what magic is all about. To be able to consciously turn the wheel of the solar plexus by will it is possible to draw in and increase the amount of energy accessible to the body. This substance, energy or vibration can then be directed out of the body again by will, as in the case of healing or even distant healing. The effect of using crystals as amplifiers of this energy can be extremely powerful and by choosing the correct crystal or mineral, in the shape of a wand to direct healing energy to a specific area, can have amazing results. It is through this energy centre that man is able to draw in everything from the universe. Remembering, of course, that everything in the universe is either negative or positive – nothing remains neutral. It either nourishes or poisons – it is black or white.

The solar plexus is often considered to be the 'magical'

centre. Once this wheel is set in motion by a person's consciousness and directed toward a certain goal, their reticular action takes over and, without further conscious direction, continues to execute the deed until it's completed. For this reason some say that, once knowingly used, 'innocence can no longer be yours'. Once you have passed through this gate you can no longer say 'I didn't understand'. Many never activate this centre because they are fearful. They are afraid of what they could be or become. They are afraid to take responsibility for their own path, preferring to go round and round in circles rather then face the fearful 'guardian of the gate' – Malkuth – according to the kabbalah. Known as the 'tenth sephiroth' and placed at the base of the pillar of equilibrium, students of this ancient text believe that Malkuth holds the gate to the Garden of Eden or, as we might relate to it – this physical world. Malkuth represents the psychic aspects of matter and is said to be the 'Earth soul' or, on the tree of life, the sphere of Earth. Malkuth represents the elements of earth, air, fire and water as the four conditions in which energy can exist. Malkuth represents the Earth Mother and is the gateway to other worlds, for the womb of the Mother is the gate to life. It is also the gate to death – for birth, into the form of matter, is sometimes death to higher forms.

3

The
chakras

The chakra colours – and the body

There are many energy centres on the body and each relates to
and is affected by each other. There are minor centres in the
joints, more important centres in the hands and feet and
many along the spinal column. I have heard it said, by our
friends amongst the native American elders, that there are three
hundred and sixty four energy centres on the body. I would not

be surprised to learn that there are three hundred and sixty five, one for each day of the year. The ones that are most written about are seven centres located along the spine and up through the head. There are basically three lower centres, believed to relate to the physical body, and three higher centres believed to relate to the spiritual body. The centre in the middle is believed to be the bridge between those two worlds.

These energy centres, in an ideal state, spin clockwise at similar rates. They should be in balance with, and relate to, each other. When under stress etc. some will spin erratically. Not only in their speed but also by 'wobbling' out of control. Under certain conditions these same centres could also spin anti-clockwise as in cases of severe stress.

The base chakra

The usual colour for this is red – which is the lowest vibration in the rainbow spectrum. This chakra deals primarily with the survival instinct and the reptilian brain. Hence it would relate to the immune system, the stiffness of joints, anaemia and lethargy. It controls the organs and glands relevant to the area at the base of the spine, the genitals, intestinal and bowel system and the gonads. These glands are known to affect our personality.

The sacral chakra

The usual colour for this is orange, the second colour in the rainbow spectrum. This chakra is also referred to as the 'abdominal' centre and deals with all our relationships in life. Hence it would relate to the adrenal glands, which give us adrenaline, energy or the ability to absorb shock. It is also the seat of sexual energy and is where people store 'chi' or life force.

The solar plexus chakra

The usual colour for this is yellow, the third colour in the rainbow spectrum. This is probably the most crucial centre on the body in relation to deciding the balance of power. This is because it is the centre of power. Power that relates to emotional energy and, when used in the wrong way, selfishness and domination prevail. This is seen where the vortices of energy spin anticlockwise and pull all the energy in towards themselves. In a lesser sense this can also be 'clingy' people who desperately need to be loved because they cannot feel the essence of love coming from their heart and so draw energy from those around them. This is when the centre is erratic or inverted. It is the centre that should normally be quiescent, a still reflection of the heart. In the physical body, it relates to the pancreas, stomach and the intestines. It relates to the process of absorbing 'prana' or life energy from food. Also, in a positive sense, it releases toxins from the body and, therefore, deals with transmutation in its highest aspect. It is often referred to as the 'fight or flight' centre. Anxiety and fear are acknowledged here and is where 'thought becomes action' or, when internalised, inaction – resulting in disharmony in the liver and pancreas etc.

The heart chakra

The usual colour for this is green, the fourth colour in the rainbow spectrum. It relates to the factor of love and in balance, its counterpart, wisdom. When this centre is out of balance it moves downward – to the solar plexus. It starts to spin the wrong way, leading to an involuntary movement downward. Physically, it relates to the thymus gland and, when it's in balance, it stimulates the immune system. It frees us from the domination of others and supports the development of our own thoughts and values. When it is in total balance it also opens up another centre, above the heart and below the throat chakra, called the thymus centre. This is otherwise known as the body 'bodhisattva' point or 'point of enlightenment'. The heart chakra is positioned between the three lower and three higher chakras and acts as the link between the physical and spiritual aspects of a person – often referred to as 'the bridge'.

The throat chakra

The usual colour for this is blue, the fifth colour of the rainbow spectrum. This is the centre that deals with 'active' intelligence and communication. It assists with painkilling and brings calm when in balance. It encourages patience and uplifts and clarifies the mind. It also represents truth. When it spins the wrong way the energy is projected down into the sacral centre and then what you think about and feel and the words that you speak become related only to personality and desire. One of these lower aspects is money and materialism because money is essentially a form of communication. When balanced it would translate to caring and sharing. Physically it would relate to the thyroid gland which encourages cell growth. It is also important to the glandular system bringing harmony to the body and helping to reduce blood pressure.

The brow chakra

The usual colour related to this is indigo, the sixth colour of the rainbow spectrum. This centre is relevant to vision and, many believe, our perception of truth. Its quality is to see things as they really are. It is the centre of creative visualisation and can gather information from our higher self. When there is an imbalance in this centre it will project psychic conflict into the outside world. Physically, it corresponds to the pituitary gland and relates to our self-worth and any form of disharmony within our self-image. When in balance it would relate to growth and balance throughout the body.

The crown chakra

The usual colour related to this is violet and is the seventh colour of the rainbow spectrum.

This centre is known as the 'thousand petalled lotus' or the 'seat of the soul'. This is because the crown contains seven centres that correspond to the seven body centres and it is called the rainbow bridge, often seen in the aura as bright white light or golden rays.

Physically this centre relates to the pineal gland which regulates the function of all the endocrine organs through the hormone melatonin. Melatonin is produced to sedate the endocrine organs when they become overactive or stressed. It also has an effect on brain activity. People who complain of their brain being tired could have melatonin to thank for it. When their metabolism races, melatonin steps in to sedate excess overactivity with a feeling of sleepiness – thus resting the other endocrine organs of the body. When the body requires extra melatonin the metabolism is slowed and brain activity is quietened. It is in this state that more frequent experiences of psychic phenomena have been reported. There is also evidence to suggest a relationship between melatonin and the presence of electromagnetic fields (EMFs). This gland seems to require light to function properly and, consequently, is affected by the rhythms of the Sun and Moon – which appear to relate to our 'biological clock'. The crown chakra cannot function effectively until the personality is relatively balanced.

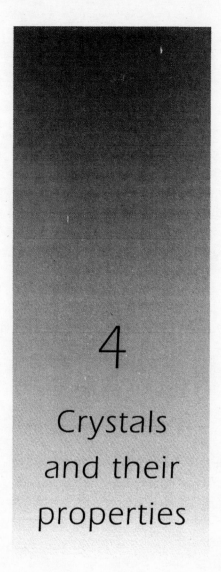

4

Crystals and their properties

Over my years as a crystal healer, I suppose the most frequently asked questions I get relate to crystals and their properties. In the shop I see a procession of people wandering around the shelves clutching either a book or a 'crystal identity chart' – but they still feel they have to ask for advice. Remember that the relationships we form with crystals are individual. Generally, crystals' properties are consistent – no matter who uses them – but you will find that different people may react slightly differently to the same crystal. As a healer, you will certainly find that some crystals will work better for you than others. Even individual specimens can exhibit slight differences. So my advice is, if you don't feel that you're getting the response you expect from an individual stone, try other samples of the same crystal. It can take quite a while to build up a collection of crystals that work for you – so don't get discouraged. It takes patience and perseverance (that sounds like something my mother might have said) but it's well worth the effort.

Over the last 18 years I have been using crystals for healing. I have always tried to keep notes of their effects and the reactions they have elicited. I have edited my notes into the following list. It doesn't pretend to be comprehensive, but it does cover what I have found to be the most commonly used crystals and minerals. You might want to start your own list – I still add to mine.

Agate. A form of chalcedony which naturally forms in bands of beautiful colours. It occurs as a cavity filling in lava and can often have wonderful crystals growing inside. An Agate Geode, immersed in dye before cutting, produces random absorption of colour. When they are cut and polished the finished product looks spectacular. There are many colours of Agate, each having a slightly different vibration. Agate provides for the balancing of yin-yang energy and is therefore a good overall healing stone that brings balance to all parts of the body. It is a stone that helps create a bridge between the physical and the etheric bodies, seeking truth and courage within. It can aid in lifting depression by opening the door to understanding. It is both energising and grounding. The lymphatics, the pancreas and the circulatory system all benefit from this mineral by stabilising the aura from the heart chakra downward grounding dysfunctional energies.

Sit quietly with your arms resting on either side of your body. Experiment with holding two different Agate stones, one in each hand. Try, perhaps, a Green Agate and a Black Agate. Swap hands after a few minutes and try again. The sensations will vary. Keep a note of any sensations you feel and continue to try a variety of Agates as and when you acquire them. In time you will build up a pattern of the ones that work best for you. Some combinations will ground you while others will stimulate movement within the chakras. Use them as your personal medicine kit.

Amazonite. This feldspar mineral is generally used to help soothe the nervous system and balance the metabolism. It gives relief to those suffering from emotional and mental stress. Once the nerves and the metabolic rate are more under control the body can think more clearly allowing us to express ourselves creatively. It relieves the feelings of guilt by giving perspective to our most harmful traits and helping us to 'let go'.

Amber. Amber is a resin, mainly found in the Baltic region and the Dominican Republic. Sicily produces a small amount, but not much of that finds it way to the United Kingdom. Considered a 'mystical' resin, it was used by the ancients as a 'hex-breaker' and healer. It is traditionally worn around the throat chakra to relieve asthma, convulsions and bronchial disorders. Used for the alleviation of pain from rheumatism, intestinal problems, bladder trouble and earache.

Able to absorb negative energies, Amber can trigger the mind into remembering the soul. In ancient times, particularly to the people of 'the craft' throughout the United Kingdom and Europe, this fossilised resin was a favourite material for amulets – worn as protection from the 'evil eye'. It was believed to have the power to protect from danger of the plague and a large piece would be worn on the throat chakra to prevent nasal catarrh, hay fever and asthma. Many 'high priests' and 'priestesses' even today will wear amber beads interspersed with jet for their magical properties.

Amber, in its rough state, is also used as an ingredient in incense for rituals of love and healing. As an oil it is extremely thick in consistency with a camphor-like odour. It is usually mixed with a carrier oil to dilute its strength and used to rub or massage onto the body to relieve aches and pains. It is rare to find true amber oil. Jewellery quality amber is often boiled when the tiny droplets of water trapped within expand and fan out to make attractive designs in the clear resin. Occasionally, tiny insects become trapped within the resin. Needless to say, these samples can be extremely valuable.

Amethyst. The Purple Quartz, Amethyst is considered to exude 'female' properties. Admired for its beauty, this semi-precious stone is known for its spirituality and used extensively for healing and meditation. It is said by mystics that sleeping with Amethyst can promote intuitive dreams and astral travel. However only the pure of heart can bring that knowledge back with them. It can strengthen the immune system and aid both the pituitary and pineal glands. It is, therefore, an exceptionally good blood cleanser. This powerful crystal facilitates trans-mutation of lower energies into the higher frequencies of both the spiritual and ethereal levels.

Ametrine. A fairly recent discovery – Ametrine occurs when seams of Amethyst and Citrine overlap each other. This unique stone carries the attributes of both the 'parent' crystals. Healers believe that the Earth mysteries have entwined the male energy of Citrine and the female energy of Amethyst to form the beauty of Ametrine. It is believed to strengthen the immune system, regenerating and recharging the physical body. It is believed to be an exceptional blood cleanser and energiser, ridding the bloodstream of unwanted toxins. It clears the head from stress and tension allowing great focus for meditation. It is an 'opener' of the 'third eye' – inspiring healing and divination.

Angelite. Known as the 'awareness' stone – Angelite is a very dense mineral that, whilst enhancing telepathic communication, helps us to gain more control. It is particularly good for maintaining a contact with reality while we allow our spiritual awareness to make its journeys. It appears to accelerate both the speed and clarity of telesomatic activity by allowing a finer degree of 'sympathetic vibration' or 'attunement'. It is a highly effective stone for healers since it both enhances their perceptions of the ailment in question and, at the same time, keeps the healer in touch with the here and now. For those embarking on their spiritual journey, Angelite is a very valuable friend.

Apatite. The use of Apatite can help to stabilise activity by balancing the chakras and clearing blockages. It has proved useful in dealing with hyperactive children and autistic children alike. It has great success in raising the base energy and releases sexual frustration by giving one permission to lust as well as to love without feelings of guilt. Apatite also works on the suppression of hunger and raising of the metabolic rate.

Apophyllite. Quality specimens and grades of Apophyllite occur predominantly in Poona, India. They primarily appear in green/white or clear/colourless forms. I have found these to be of extremely good quality, not only for their energies but also for their outstanding beauty. Under the umbrella of Apophyllites I have learnt a tremendous amount about the energies of Prehnite, Silbites and Dolomite. All seem to be related and I have found Apophyllite a good teacher. It is used to create a conscious connection between the physical form and the spiritual realms. It can facilitate astral travel and provide a clear connection to the physical body during the travel. It allows us to send information we have gathered back to the conscious self. When placed in a room, Apophyllite seems to create its own presence that attracts and holds your attention – and each time you admire it, you will find something new in it. It works well as a receiver of spiritual connections. It seems to almost attract the attention of the higher realms – and has even been known to bring glimpses of the akashic record. I love this mineral and all it has to offer, a great addition to anyone's collection. It is interesting to note that it is often the first one to which children are drawn.

Aqua Aura is clear or cloudy quartz crystal – enhanced by a coating of 24ct gold which adheres to the natural electro-magnetic field of the crystal. The refraction of light through the crystal and the gold gives the effect of a beautiful blue hue. The wonderful energy of these two components amplifies the properties of each. It opens the throat chakra and can be been used effectively to activate the energy of other crystals. Healers find it most useful in the cleansing of the aura, where it helps to identify damaged or distressed areas. The spiritual body can also benefit from the way this advanced combination can release blockages in the fibres that connect us to the super energy.

Aquamarine. This stone provides us with the courage to be calm, whatever the circumstance, and consider our actions. It attunes to our highest spiritual level of awareness and works towards the highest good. Like a she-wolf prowling around her cubs, this stone keeps us spiritually awake. It protects us during the travelling, exploration and understanding of the inner child. This stone activates and cleanses the throat chakra enabling a clear channel for the process of trance-mediumship. It is useful in the treatment of swollen glands and the clearing of stress-related pressure behind the eyes.

Aragonite. Aragonite can be a great help in preparing for meditation and healing. It calms the physical body whilst lifting the vibration, allowing spiritual communication to take place. This rise in the vibration can be felt throughout the body, bringing warmth to the extreme energy centres of the hands and feet. It is a teacher of discipline and responsibility. It encourages patience and acceptance. Aragonite is good for those who push themselves too far and need to accept that sometimes it's alright to delegate.

Aventurine. The most common colour for Aventurine is green, although it is also found in a salmon-red or blue. When it's polished, the surface has a sort of gleam about it from the Mica or Hematite content. It is used to balance the heart chakra and is considered to be a protector of the two worlds – the etheric and the physical. It is often associated with the zodiac sign Libra – the scales – since it 'weighs and balances' the alignment of the intellectual and the emotional bodies. It is believed to have the ability to shut down either as appropriate. It relieves the tension of migraine headaches and soothes the eyes.

Azurite. Reputed to be the stone that opens the 'third eye', Azurite aids our understanding of psychic experiences and our ability to verbalise them. It is said that meditating with this crystal can access the channels of thought transferral allowing communication between physical and ethereal beings. It is also regarded as an excellent tool in the development of astral travel. Used as a healing stone it relieves arthritis, back pain, stress from worrying, spasms and fits, sadness and sorrowfulness. Tell your troubles to the Azurite crystal and suddenly they don't seem so bad – before long you can't even remember them and life seems altogether more rosy.

Bismuth. This remarkable family of minerals comes in a number of forms that all share, broadly, the same properties. It is widely believed to relieve the feelings of isolation that we inevitably feel in the pursuit of our spiritual path. It prepares us for the acceptance and realisation that no one is going to do it for us and there is no greater mentor than 'source'. We must each walk our own path and find our own way. There are as many paths as there are people and sometimes along the way we stumble across a soul mate with whom experiences have been shared in another time. The feelings are not so much a sudden realisation as a 'knowing' but we undoubtedly recognise them – and, for a while, we walk a 'parallel path'. Our yearning for understanding and companionship allows our emotions to run away with us and our spiritual path stops. The danger arises when one of us gives too much of our power to the other and we stop taking responsibility for our own path. This is when a positive changes to a negative. Bismuth teaches us not to fall asleep along our path. We learn how to identify the situation and take our power back without disrupting the relationship.

Bloodstone. The mineral Bloodstone is a member of the Jasper family and is associated with many gifts. It is believed to have mystical attributes that can enable us to take control of spirit energies, dispel evil and banish negativity. It improves our sense of creativity, decision making and intuition. It is an excellent grounding tool and, placed in a dish of water next to the bed, will assure a peaceful night's sleep. Remember to flush the water away in the morning and replace it with fresh, cold water ready for another peaceful night. It has been used in the treatment of leukaemia, purifying the blood and clearing toxins. It aids the functions of the liver, intestines and bladder, and relates to the sacral and heart chakras.

Boji Stone. The Boji Stone is a registered trademark from the Rocky Mountains of the USA. It is usually a dark brown spherical shape. Some are smooth and regarded as having a female or negative energy. Others are more pitted with a rim around the middle and are considered to have a male or positive energy. They are used in the balancing of the male/female energies and alignment of the chakras. I have found them useful for removing energy blockages and repairing holes within the aura. Similar stones, used in the same way and identical in mineralogical terms, are known as Moqui-Marbles or Ironstone Nodules.

Bornite – Peacock Ore. This amazingly coloured stone can range from a tarnished red-brown through to blue, turquoise, purple and yellow in colour. It is often called the 'grief stone'. If we find ourselves attracted to it, the subconscious may be subtly nudging us to let go of someone or something. This mineral acts like a breath of fresh air blowing away the cobwebs and sweeping the house clean in readiness and anticipation for a new visitor. It makes room for fun to enter our life and give us a lift. It puts a sparkle back in our eye and stimulates the spirit to explore its higher limits. It is considered to be a great protector from negative energy and works on the upper chakras.

Calcite. Calcite is crystalline calcium carbonate largely formed from the shells of sea organisms that build over time into limestone. After even more time it is transformed again into marble. It can be found at the core of many rocks. Calcite is found worldwide and is fluorescent, sometimes even transparent or translucent. Its association with foreign atoms and minerals cause drastic colour variations and dilutions of character. It is often compared to the spiritual evolution of mankind as both go through many transformations along their journey. As a variety of coloured stone, it benefits the kidneys, pancreas and spleen. Calcite alleviates fear and stress. It is considered to be a balancer of the male and female energies. It helps us to gain our composure and gives us control over our emotions. It can encourage us to simply 'be' in order to receive inspiration and guidance. It assists decision making and clarifies dreams, visions and channelling.

Blue Calcite is the gentle Calcite. It works on the throat chakra, giving clarity of speech and aiding the verbalisation of thought. The structure of the mineral absorbs energy and appears to act as a filter returning that energy to the sender without the 'static', thus the sender is calmer yet stronger.

Green Calcite is often used on the body just below the heart chakra and works on the adrenal glands, the nervous system, the digestion and all bacterial growth infections. It is also renowned for its success in dealing with mental fears, soothing anxieties and grounding chaotic energies.

Red Calcite works on the base chakra – dealing with vitality and the physical will to survive. It also relieves constipation and acts on pain and stress relating to the lower spinal column.

Orange Calcite aids the gall bladder and the reproductive organs. It works on the balance of the emotions and on the acquisition of wisdom.

Aqua Calcite works on the breathing, the lungs and life force. Its energy is cleansing and calming. It stimulates ideas and logic, pushing us to expand our goals and achievements.

Honey Calcite attunes to the higher realms, channelling the healing rays directly from source. It lifts grey areas from within the aura and works well on the alleviation of depression. A good all round healer.

Mango Calcite is believed to commune with the angelic realms and allow us to glimpse behind the 'veil'. The love energy is strong within this stone and teaches us much about our own needs and wants. It permits us to think of ourselves without guilt as it is only when we are at our best that we can give of our best.

Optical Calcite improves the functions of the eyes, soothing the nerves behind the eyes and grounding the tensions that grow into migraine headaches if not checked.

Dog-Tooth Calcite is a stubborn, unmoving crystal, excellent when you need reserve and inner strength. A piece placed on your desk or your working area prevents you from being walked over or disregarded. It is a crystal that demands respect and caution.

Black Calcite is considered the crystal of regression and memory. It aids us with the memory and acts as a record keeper. It keeps us grounded and has a reputation for returning us to our body after trauma or immense stress.

Carnelian. Provides perception and awakens our talents by channelled inspiration. It is an excellent stone for day-dreamers because it sharpens the concentration and helps absentmindedness. It dispels apathy and mental lethargy. As a healing tool Carnelian works on all the chakras below the heart and is useful in the treatment of rheumatism, arthritis and neuralgia. It attacks the depression that is brought on by the reality of advancing years and is useful in the treatment of infertility and impotence. It gives us understanding of our cycles and rhythms and helps us to accept our individuality. As a mystical stone it is said that placing a piece of Carnelian above each opening of the home will protect you from psychic attack and return negativity to whence it came.

Celestine. Known as the 'teacher', Celestine is widely believed to have the ability to 'jump-start' awareness of the higher self. It is widely used by those starting out on their path of self-discovery, or by those who may have become lost, to recover higher consciousness. Celestine promotes awareness and sensitivity of the etheric self by identifying troubled parts of the aura and restoring balance. Celestine reveals truths, engendering reliability and clarity in thought and speech.

Chrysocolla. The 'woman's friend', Chrysocolla is widely believed to relieve menstrual and premenstrual stresses and pain. It strengthens feminine qualities in both genders. Amongst healers it is widely accepted that Chrysocolla helps in the prevention of ulcers and digestive problems. It also relieves arthritic pain, toughens the lungs and thyroid glands while stabilising and enhancing the metabolism. It alleviates guilt, tensions and phobias while inspiring creativity, personal power, joy and serenity.

Chrysoprase. This mineral is associated with the sacral chakra or the second chakra and is therefore used to treat fertility problems, the digestive system, the goitre, gonads and the hormones. It is sometimes considered one of the most sensitive areas in the body as it is the pathway by which reincarnation takes place. This stone can open the doorways to the universe and access life-giving energies from source. Some say that it can even heal a broken heart. It will encourage forgiveness, allowing us to let go and move on.

Citrine. Often referred to as Burnt Amethyst, Citrine is a mineral that does not hold negative energy. Citrine is able to take negativity and ground it, returning it to whence it came. Hence it never needs to be cleansed. This crystal works on the solar plexus chakra. It communicates on the etheric as an early warning system, alerting us that self-protection is necessary and allowing us to place barriers before an attack. This healing crystal can aid digestion and disorders of the stomach. It has also been used for visual problems, tenacity, to activate the thymus and to balance the thyroid. It is a stone for regeneration and recharge. It attracts what is needed – which is not always what is wanted. Citrine eliminates destructive tendencies by raising the self-esteem. It brings cheer and a light heart, hope, warmth and energy to all who work in the energy of this beautiful crystal. It is widely considered a crystal of male or positive energies and is often placed beside a female crystal, such as Amethyst, to balance energy fields between them. When used in configuration healings it is placed in the East, the position of fire and the home of intuition.

Copal. Copal gum is the North American equivalent of frankincense native to Mexico and gathered from the hills of the Sonora Desert. It was considered to be food for the souls of departed spirits and an offering to the gods. Copal is still used to cleanse objects and exorcise places. It has been used in magical ceremonies for thousands of years and believed to have been the incense of the Mayans. It is pale to dark yellow in colour and burns with a sweet citrus perfume. It is used in rituals of protection, purification, exorcism and spirituality. Healers will often make small pouches of natural fabric or skin in which to keep a few grams of Copal. They will wear it around there neck or place it under their pillow to ward off negative energies.

Copper. Copper is used for its conductive qualities to ground static energy and to relieve rheumatism and arthritis. It is also said to stabilise blood flow and balance body fluids. Copper is quite successful in balancing the base and sacral chakras as well as pulling the etheric and physical bodies together after times of stress. It is often used to conduct the energy of the healer into the patient via crystals which amplify the electrical impulses in the exchange of energy. Many specialised wands are constructed from Copper to provide good conductivity between the wand's crystals and the healer. It is known to combat sleeping sickness and lethargy just by wearing it as a bangle. Don't worry about your skin going green – the faster it does the more effective it will be. Plumbers' copper coils made into rings of about 30cms across make an excellent protection from environmental electro-magnetic fields when placed around the home on offending windows or walls. For those who are sensitive to the emanations of TV or computers' cathode ray tubes (CRTs) one of these coils placed between you and the screen will act as a protective screen, enabling you to watch a few programmes at the very least.

Dioptase. This beautiful green stone is not a common mineral, found in oxidised parts of copper sulphide deposits in only a few locations. It is mainly found in North Africa and, in more recent years, Russia. It is regarded by healers as one of the best healing stones of the age. I have found it to be a majestic and dramatic mineral that can have a powerful effect on human energy fields. It is full of self-importance and brings to our attention the 'here and now'. This exquisite crystal works especially well on the heart chakra, helping it align the solar plexus by 'pulling' it upwards towards the fulfilment of aspirations realised. With this energy we can reach deep into our own resources and handle anything with a positive attitude. Addictions, emotions, stress, health, finances. Changes negatives to positives – now.

Dolomite. The 'giving' stone, Dolomite is believed to encourage charitable actions and foster the selfless consciousness required for healing. It encourages impulsive, original thinking and is widely used as an aid to energy realignment. It is used by healers to strengthen bones, teeth and the physical structure – bringing weaker parts of the body into line with the whole.

Dumortierite. Granular or fibrous masses in blue to violet and pink to brown. The blue to violet, in particular, is excellent for stimulating the ability to verbalise our spiritual experiences. It guides us to the realisation that all we consider to be real is, in fact, an illusion and what we consider to be illusion is real. Reality is purely a matter of perception and, as we shift our awareness, we change our 'reality'. Dumortierite grounds the overexcited and turns that energy into a positive mental attitude for all situations. It restores composure and roots us firmly to the physical, while still allowing the spiritual to come through.

Emerald. The 'stone of successful love', Emerald provides the balance necessary within a relationship and helps to keep it constant. It makes a wonderful addition to an engagement or eternity ring. It proclaims unconditional love. It can be used to enhance the memory and to stimulate greater mental capacity. The Emerald helps to combine intelligence with discernment, allowing for the choice of 'right' action to be the only choice available. It can be used to open, activate and stimulate the heart chakra, while helping to quiet the emotions. It is a stone that brings harmony to all areas of our life.

Fluorite. This mineral is most associated with progress and growth and has the ability to make one 'more'. Fluorite promotes relaxation and peace of mind. It is a natural healer. Fluorine, a component of fluorite, is said to influence the structure and strength of the human body. A smooth piece of tumbled superior Fluorite stroked across the skin in the direction of the heart relieves pain. It can be particularly useful in the treatment of rheumatism and arthritis. It will also aid the healing of skin tissue, wrinkles and blemishes. There is an old wives' tale that Fluorite held next to the sinuses will relieve cold and 'flu symptoms. As the crystal warms during a healing it is absorbing negative energies – the stress that is causing the problem. The crystal will need to be washed in cold water to cleanse and cool it regularly. Fluorite comes from the Latin word 'fluo', to flow, pour, stream. This is believed to be because Fluorite melts with ease and is used to assist fusion when smelting with other metals. The ability to change and alter its condition by melting allows it to become more than itself. It makes a wonderful teacher by its example.

Fuchsite. Fuchsite, when used in channelling, can bring us information concerning natural and herbal holistic remedies. When Fuchsite is used in conjunction with other minerals, during healing sessions, it can promote an increase in energy transfer. It has the unusual property of 'shifting' energy to the points where it appears lowest. It can remove the excess energy from blockages and transfer it, as positive energy, to where it is needed most. It is very successful in helping with spinal alignment, muscular flexibility and balancing blood cells.

Galena is a lead ore. It is a dense and heavy mineral that has a metallic finish to its octahedral structure. Galena is a good for grounding and is often used to enhance the balancing of energies. It makes a connection between the ethereal and physical, stimulating an alignment of energy. It is a 'stone of harmony' stimulating interaction on all levels and the decrease of self-limiting ideas. It can aid the stimulation of hair growth and strengthen the lungs, thyroid and nervous system. Galena should never be taken internally, even in an elixir.

Garnet. Known as the 'daydreamer', Garnet is believed to regenerate body systems – especially the bloodstream where it is also a good purifier. It is also strongly associated with the balancing of sex drive and emotional disharmony. It can bring love, compassion and an enhanced imagination. It helps to strengthen those who willingly attune to it and wear it. It can warn of approaching danger and forces us to make honourable commitments and decisions.

Geode. Geodes are hollow, round stone formations lined with a mineral, most often a Quartz. Although Geodes have some of the properties of the mineral that line the interior, they also have qualities of their own. Generally, Geodes are a catalyst for action, movement and manifestation. They bring healing, intensity and warmth. Geodes are good for relieving lethargy. They stimulate energy and brain activity. The lesson of the Geode is that even something that could be considered ugly on the outside has beauty. Grown deep within the Earth Mother, the male energies of the Geode, once found and opened, affect our perception. It offers us the realisation that, if you desire movement in your life, you have to be the one prepared to move. The energies are circular in movement, creating a balancing and calming effect on both the aura and the physical body, allowing movement to start from a centred being.

Gold. Used by the Egyptians for empowerment, this wondrous metal has been used to bind people together for centuries. It is said that Yellow Gold is used in wedding rings for this reason. This could explain why more people are now using White Gold – so that neither can dominate the other. Gold is used also to empower magical talisman and symbols. For centuries it has been thought to attract the attention of the gods. Gold imbues us with the energy and vitality of the Sun – positive and vibrant. Used to balance the heart chakra and open the third eye, it is also believed to attune us, through the crown chakra, to natural universal energy. It is often used as a conductor of energy, wrapped around healing wands or as a coating for Copper used in the same way. It can aid all chakras and is referred to as a master healer.

Granite. A strange mineral which goes through alternating periods of popularity and obscurity. Used by the ancient people of the Maya and native Americans in much the same way as Diorite. As a protecting or magical mineral it can have cavities inside its textured mass producing Quartz crystals and was often used as a connection to the Earth Mother. It can often break down into more common clay minerals, such as Kaolin, which are powdered and taken internally for stomach disorders. It is used in meditation enabling us to recognise the difference between a psychic experience or just wishful thinking.

Gypsum. See Selenite.

Hematite. Hematite takes its name from the Greek word for 'blood' which is descriptive of the colour seen in powdered Hematite. This is a stone that most healers will not do without. It works extremely well at restoring, strengthening and regulating the blood flow. Hands, crippled from bad circulation, seem to respond to holding a piece of Hematite. In fact there are many who take a piece to bed with them to hold while they drift off to sleep. Sufferers of cramp and spasms notice an immediate improvement in their health just by having it touch their skin. Keep a couple of pieces in your pocket and tumble them like worry beads. Hematite grounds negative energies that manifest as stress. It releases us from compulsive habits like drinking, over-eating and smoking – and from nervous obsessive behaviour.

Herkimer Diamond. The ultimate 'attunement stone', Herkimer Diamonds are used to attune oneself to another person, environment or activity. Herkimers are frequently given as a keepsake to someone travelling or moving away – to keep them attuned to those left behind. Herkimers are widely believed to have a 'memory' that can store information for retrieval later. It is also common for healers to use Herkimers to begin the first session with a new subject – in order to attune the consciousness of each. The Herkimer stimulates clairvoyance, prescience and telepathic abilities. If two Herkimers are held together, between two people, and then one kept by each of them, the stones will retain their attunement no matter how far they are separated – thus maintaining a link between the two holders. Original Herkimer Diamonds are from the area around Herkimer, New York – but lately, there has been a flood of 'counterfeits' – Clear Quartz stones from areas like India and Africa. The unique clarity and properties of a genuine Herkimer are believed to stem from the way they grow – nestling in the fast-flowing waters of the rivers flowing into Niagara Falls.

Howlite. White Howlite has a soothing pulse and is excellent in the use of insomnia. It slows the activity of the mind and allows undisturbed rest. Blue Howlite goes one further by allowing us to recall our dreams and bring back the wisdom from them. It is used in the teachings of patience and aids memory expansion. Howlite can eliminate rage and calm violent, uncontrolled anger. Keep it in your pocket or on your person to absorb negative energies. It will prove a great help in controlling your own anger and will soften anger directed at you.

Jade. Associated with wisdom and music, Jade is used to enhance the focus in prayer and ceremony and allows us access to knowledge like that used in the ancient rituals of the Mayan culture. It radiates the feelings of tranquillity, kindness, nurturing and love. Jade aids fertility and eases childbirth. It brings serenity and peace. It calms aggressive problems of the hips, kidneys and spleen and balances the heart chakra. Jade is said to attract good luck, friendship, loyalty and protection on long journeys.

Jasper. Jasper is a chalcedony comprised of minute Quartz crystals with sub-microscopic pores. It comes in a wide variety of colours, even some with stripes or spots. Mainly, the family of Jasper assist in grounding to a greater or lesser degree.

Brecciated Jasper. This variation is very good for placing one's feet firmly on the ground and emotional composure. It takes the static feeling away from the crown chakra allowing clarity of thought.

Picture Jasper is said to be the great Earth Mother speaking to us. Those who are aware can read her messages in the pictures. It has a slow pulse and some say they can hear her laughter whilst meditating with this stone. It helps one to face hidden thoughts, feelings of guilt, envy, pity, hatred or love. Brings things to the surface that need to be dealt with and helps us to realise that they are just lessons to learn along the way and we can laugh with the Earth Mother. Picture Jasper alleviates fear and brings comfort to those who feel vulnerable. All you need do is hold this magical crystal.

Red Jasper makes a good worry bead and a few tumbled in the pocket have a surprisingly remarkable effect on our emotions. It provides insight into the most difficult of problems. It helps stabilise the energy field around the body and has a cleansing effect on the aura.

Jet. Jet is a very hard form of natural carbon – close, in mineral composition, to coal. It is, in fact, fossilised wood from the 'monkey-puzzle tree'. It is used for protection and is known as the 'stone of the witches'. Worn around the neck, usually with Amber, it protects from the entities of darkness, against illness and violence. There is a lot of superstition surrounding this mineral and it is said that those attracted to it are 'old souls'.

During circle work it is believed that wearing Jet guards the physical body allowing safe spiritual travelling.

Kunzite. I find that working with Kunzite subtly restructures the molecules that make up the physical body. It appears to have a calming effect on the metabolism and is therefore able to balance out panic attacks and periods of deep stress-related anxiety. We all have times of being 'out of sorts' and that is fine as long as we spring back out of them. But when we feel angry and lack self worth, the atoms that make up the physical body meet with resistance, preventing them from springing back into shape. It is then that Kunzite makes an excellent healer and its vibration calmly dissolves any negative build up. It instils a sense of peace and tranquillity, producing a shield of protection around the aura and leaving us space within to heal. Kunzite works on the heart chakra.

Kyanite. Kyanite forms as fibrous masses in long blades – some twisted but mostly straight. The Blue Kyanite is used for healing and strengthening the throat and larynx. It is well known as a friend to singers and performers. It aligns all chakras naturally and is particularly successful with the crown, third eye and throat chakras. The blades of Kyanite allow us to cut through illusion by working within the dimensions that structure one's thinking. After a healing, using this technique, one feels emotionally lighter and suddenly more creative as if the 'ki' energy connection has been restored. Some people will wear a Kyanite pendant to help them keep in balance and will intuitively find themselves holding the pendant when a surge of 'ki' energy is required. It acts like a signal to 'source' that aid is needed, and works by the conscious and subconscious sending the same signal so that will and intent become one.

Labradorite. This type of feldspar, which I came across some years ago, can look like a lump of Black Granite with sparkly blue pieces in its natural state. But, when polished, can be one of the most beautiful and mystical stones I have ever found. Healers know the value of this mineral immediately. Some believe Labradorite to be descended from the stars and the pictures seen on polished surfaces are the universes it has travelled. It is said to bring the wearer a wealth of wisdom and understanding. It is used to heal head energy and ground the activity of an overactive mind. It also aids menstrual tension and balances the hormones. It is customarily worn as a piece of jewellery around the neck and, for meditations, held in the leading hand.

Lapis Lazuli. The stone of the ancient ones, used by magicians through the ages. Powdered lazurite is a source of the ultra-marine pigment and is used in oil or egg tempera for painting. This stone is the reflection of the universe. The tiny flecks of Pyrite being the stars. Used extensively in jewellery inlay, often worn on the throat or the heart chakra. It is used for protection, bonding loved ones and friendship. The richly adorned collars and necklaces of the pharaohs were heavily inlaid with Lapis. This stone is said to be given to the children of man from the Children of God – the Angels. It is said to be a message or gift from before time began. It has the ability to give the wearer understanding of the sacred texts hidden within accessible scrolls and books which are constantly coming to light. It changes the reality of the wearer by opening a higher awareness lifting the vibration and thus connecting one to the fibres of source. Lapis placed on the brow allows insight into our dreams and can help to develop astral travel. It supports courage in working toward spiritual development. It alerts one to psychic attack and returns it 'to whence it came'. It is used for treatment of the immune system, and to strengthen the cellular structure.

Lapis Lazuli has a similar energy to the zodiac sign Sagittarius and the element of fire.

Larimar – (Blue Pectolite). I was using Larimar for a long time before I knew what it was. I never identified it because I believed it to be a Zeolite and, at the time, that was enough for me to know. When you're browsing through your favourite crystal shop, look for those labelled Zeolites and then check for the white silky, fibrous and uneven cleavages of Larimar. You may see them called Pectolites and they occur in cavities in basalt and similar rock. These can have a transparency about them which exhibit colour hues of blue, green or even red. These incredible minerals instil a sense of peace in one's home bringing a sense of calm and love. It is used for 'cellular cleansing' and helps us to believe in ourselves, ridding us of guilt or frustrations locked in the memory. It is gentle enough to be used in a nursery to calm a stressful child. Place some on a shelf in the room out of reach and do not allow dust to gather. I rinse these minerals under the cold tap to revitalise them when they become saturated.

Lepidolite. This mineral attunes to the crown, third eye, throat and heart chakras – opening and clearing blockages. Place some on different areas of the body and a slight vibration can be sensed at the locations of stress. It has most of the qualities of Quartz crystal except it cannot be programmed for the empowerment of negative and malevolent energies. It can only be utilised for our highest good and therefore makes an exceptional healer. In fact Lepidolite is totally impotent unless it is used for the power of good. Shamanic rites, extraterrestrial contact and astral travel are all reputed to benefit from its presence. Likewise, it aids and protects you when delving into the Akashic records for the thoughts of what has and will occur. Lithium, a derivative of Lepidolite, has been used as a medication in the treatment of manic depression. Lepidolite occasionally occurs in the form of Mica with a plate-like structure. In this form all its properties are amplified and it has limitless uses and powers. A huge comforter to those who suffer depression, it works hardest for those under stress. It is used in cases of anorexia, alcoholism and all addictions. It quickly becomes our conscience and support. With Lepidolite around the work place or home those niggling negatives that allow us to fail cease to exist – they simply cannot function in proximity with Lepidolite. It is a mineral that needs to be worked with and explored to discover what it can do for you.

Lodestone. Specimens of Magnetite possessing polarity are commonly referred to as Lodestone. This unusual mineral has been used for centuries in the relief of cramps and, placed at the bottom of your bed, ensures you of a trouble free night. This may be an old wives' tale and cramps are more likely to be helped by treatment with salts and minerals lacking in one's diet, but my experience is that Lodestone works well for occasional cramps and muscular spasms. I am not happy placing Lodestone directly on a chakra because I consider it more than a subtle energy. However, used in configurations placed around the body I believe it is able to pull wrong-way energy flow into right-way energy flow when used by an experienced healer.

Malachite. This mineral is a must for all healing pouches. The colour ranges from light to dark green and forms in masses, layers and rosettes. It is often used in the treatment of diabetes – by placing a piece of Malachite directly on the abdomen during a healing and then carrying some around the waist. It has been recognised as a benefit to the sufferers of epilepsy, for the relief of travel sickness and vertigo. It can protect us from the background radiation found in naturally high levels in certain areas, and enhances the immune system. Malachite raises our sensitivity and awareness of 'spirit guides', helping us to cultivate our psychic abilities. It is often found with Azurite and this combination (Malachite–Azurite) can be beautiful to behold and attune two main chakras at the same time – thethroat and solar plexus. Malachite–Azurite together are both secondary copper minerals although Azurite can sometimes form in small crystals on top of or beside the Malachite. Both are excellent conductors of energy.

Meteorite. Meteorites are divided by their mineralogy into three main groups. The first group is irons which are the largest Meteorites to have been found and consist mainly of nickel–iron alloys. Many, when broken open and treated with acid, expose a unique intra-growth of Kamacite and Taenite not normally found in terrestrial rock. The second largest group of Meteorites, which make up 90% of all recorded solid bodies found, are stones. These are subdivided into those with chondrules called Chondrites and those without, called Achondrites. The Chondrites are small spiracle bodies of other minerals. The Achondrites have a grainy texture. The smallest group are the stony–irons and make up only about 4% of the whole, consisting of nickel–iron and silicate minerals in equal quantities. Over the years there has been a lot of contradictory information concerning the energies of Meteorites. I have found no evidence of any healing qualities and must confess I lean toward the theory that Meteorites coming into our possession indicate change and not always for the better. At the time Hale-Bopp was within viewing distance, during 1997, my family and I were living in the Red Rocks of Arizona. The comet was a splendid site to behold and the warm desert evenings were spent gazing up at the sky in all its glory. In three months Hale-Bopp moved its way over head and out of view behind the Red Rocks. On our return to England I was surprised to find Hale-Bopp had now appeared in this hemisphere and was visible in our skies for another few months. It was quite an eerie experience to watch this comet and move around the globe with it – not one that I consider to be of a positive nature either. There were a lot of changes in our lives during this time – all of them unexpected. The weather also decided to do strange things. For example, one March night in Arizona – without warning snow fell and we were cut off from the town. The children loved it and it was not too cold – but it was hard to explain. On our return to England we had torrential rain for weeks and the nearby Glastonbury Festival turned quickly into a mud bath. There was nearly twice as much space debris recorded during the year and damage to satellites went up considerably. We healers also noted an increase in the amount of people struggling with their emotional lives during this period. Subtle energies had a lot to answer for in 1997, perhaps all of these things would have happened anyway – or maybe all Hale-Bopp did was to hurry things up. Legends tell us that bright lights in the heavens are messengers, foretelling of great wonders or impending doom. I do believe that comets coming so close to our atmosphere bring a surge of energy with them – and a huge amount of space debris that affects the planet and all who live on her.

Mica. Mica facilitates clarity in visions and mysticism. It allows a clear view of ourselves 'as others see us', giving us the opportunity to change the image seen by the outside world. It reduces hunger during fasting, relieves insomnia and dehydration. It can bring a sparkle to your eyes and a sheen to your hair. It aids clumsiness and the tendency to hesitate. Sometimes used in cases of obesity, it has the strength to reverse imbalances of the system to a level where the body can then naturally take over. A piece about the size of an egg, and thick enough to hold without breaking, should be gently rubbed in the hand. When your start to feel warm and in tune with the Mica, take it up to the chest and rub it gently over the skin up towards the neck as far as the collar bone. This allows the soothing energy to touch the skin and make contact with your energy. Mica forms in layers or sheets and large pieces are said to be 'books' containing energy from the memory of the 'first time'. The American Indians used Mica in the same way as we now use double glazing which can still be seen today in places like Sky City in the Acoma Pueblo of New Mexico. Legends have it that the clarity of the 'sheets' of Mica that come into one's possession are relative to the clarity of our vision – and that 'scrying' with Mica opens a window to the higher realms.

Moldavite. This meteoric substance has been the centre a huge amount of controversy and 'modern mythology'. Moldavite was believed to have fallen over what is now the Czech Republic about 14.8 million years ago and is reputed to be extra-terrestrial in origin. However science has now reached the conclusion that, since it is principally composed of silica-rich glass (which is in turn rich in alumina, potash and lime) it can be matched to other igneous and sedimentary rocks. This has led scientists to believe that it is more probably indigenous rock. The geologists say that a meteorite or comet impact caused intense heat to transform the surface rock around the site of impact. This, they say, explains the glassy, dark green appearance of these stones. Healers, however, say that the energy of Moldavite is among the most powerful in the mineral kingdom. Moldavite's high vibration can clear and open blockages in any of the chakras. It accelerates spiritual growth as well as increases our access to inner guidance. It is an excellent meditation stone, often used at the heart, third eye and crown chakras. In legend, Moldavite has been associated with the fabled stone of the Holy Grail, which was said to be an Emerald that fell from the sky.

Truly a gift from the heavens. So far, there has only been one recorded find of Moldavite and there will come a time when it has all been used up. It is primarily for this reason that over the years the price of this curious mineral has steadily risen.

Moonstone. Feminine and calming, emotional and loving, this smooth, milky mineral is said to be a reflection of the Moon goddess herself, encapsulated on Earth for the good of mankind. Used for many 'women's problems', period pains, tensions, pregnancy and breastfeeding mothers. This lunar stone helps us during change in our physical structure. It helps to balance the male-female energies and many men use this stone to get in touch with their 'feminine side'. It relates to the zodiac sign of Cancer, a water sign, and is often worn to give better control over emotions and to teach composure. One old wives' tale is that if you suck a piece of tumbled Moonstone under the tongue it will improve your memory. As a calming stone, Moonstone is often placed in drinking water and left to energise it for several hours before drinking the water. It was used as an ancient remedy in this way to combat insomnia. It has value in the treatment of shock and is used by healers in the treatment of hyperactive children. A Moonstone pendant is often given to people of a delicate nature, helping them come to terms with their psychic abilities and gifts.

Obsidian. Obsidian is the mysterious volcanic glass whose intrinsic properties include truth – by the reflection of our flaws – and clarity of vision. It gives us the ability to find a clear pathway and to navigate the changes necessary to eliminate 'dead ends' from our path. For these reasons, Obsidian has built a reputation for itself as a gemstone to be careful with as the truth can sometimes hurt. The Aztecs, and possibly the Mayas, certainly prized Obsidian highly and it has been found in many examples of their sacred jewellery and decoration. A beautiful piece of polished Rainbow Obsidian has remarkable powers to absorb negative energies within the aura and ground stress from the physical body. It is a strong protective stone which clarifies the inner state of the mind, relieving confusion and centring you with Earth energy. The benefits of Obsidian can be felt almost immediately and, by placing a piece on one's bedside table or under the pillow, seems to absorb mental stress and tensions. Because of its ability to absorb energy so quickly it can become saturated and needs to be washed under cold, running water in the morning if it is to be effective the following night. 'Apache tears' are often worn around the neck as pendants. These are usually distinguishable as tumbled pieces that are almost totally black. They form in a spiracle shape with conchoidal markings. People drawn naturally to apache tears may be surprised to find out that this is known by healers as a 'comfort' stone. It is often used by people who need to come to terms with grief or loss as well as those trying to give up something.

Mahogany Obsidian is beautiful – polished or unpolished. It resonates with the element of earth and has the quality of steadying a 'wobbly' aura. Good as a rescue stone when the sacral and solar plexus centres spin erratically. If you find Black Obsidian too overpowering then Mahogany Obsidian has similar qualities with a gentler vibration.

Snowflake Obsidian has white markings on the surface which are simply inclusions of other minerals resembling frozen snowflakes. This mineral is used on the sacral chakra as a gentle energy that allows you to be calm enough to recognise the patterns you make in your lives and identify the mistakes as well as the successes.

Opal. The Opal is a stone of mystery and has been associated with magic for centuries. It is believed to amplify one's existing powers, being best used when one is working on themselves or on their own path. It is the stone a magician would choose as the centre stone in the handle of his staff. It allows us to identify imperfections in our character and work on changing our nature in order to remedy them. It can be used to purify the blood, benefiting in particular the kidneys and pancreas, and can also assist in the recovery of Parkinson's disease. It is a useful identification stone when dealing with early cancers and treatment thereof.

Fire Opal is a well respected stone that should be treated with caution and anticipation. It is the symbol of hope and enhances our personal power. Often associated with the zodiac sign of Leo, and sharing the same energy, it is believed to return our feelings and thoughts to us threefold.

Opalite. Opalite initiates a deep inner cleansing where negativity has become 'lodged' in the sacral area, covering desire, emotion, creativity, sexuality and intuition. As blockages loosen it may cause flatulence, diarrhoea or even sickness but you should be prepared to persevere until balance is restored.

Peridot. Known as the 'release' stone, Peridot helps us to allow ourselves to let go of unnecessary burdens or baggage. It teaches us that the guilt that has been making us hold on to something or someone is simply an illusion of our own making. It is believed to be an excellent antitoxin gemstone. It cleans most organs and glands and is a good overall tonic for the body and mind. It reduces stress, accelerates personal growth, stimulates the mind and opens new levels of awareness and opportunity whilst banishing lethargy and laziness. It lessens the feelings of anger and jealousy and is often used to treat major organs like the heart and lungs. It has been used to aid sufferers of Chrohn's disease. Peridot works at its best on those who have gone

through a total cleansing and learnt to move on. It brings clarity
– allowing renewal to take place. The North Star is said to pull
the energies of Peridot and, like the Star, one can use the stone
to navigate one's path.

Prehnite. The crystal to heal the healer. '*From where there was
darkness grew light and illumination, peace and calm.*' Prehnite is believed
by healers to symbolise the unconditional love necessary to heal
another. It offers serenity, dignity and a sense of wholeness. A
gift first disclosed by the 'watchers' to aid the children of men
that they may not perish. Meditating with this stone connects
you to the grid of the universe. Its pulse is believed to
communicate with the energy of the Archangel Raphael. The
'dreaming' stone – Prehnite is believed to encourage contact
with the higher self by enhancing the visualisation process. It
can be used to multiply energies and to enhance our protective
fields. It is also believed to enhance the ability to prophesy – by
calling on the aid of the divine. Prehnite is excellent in dealing
with nightmares and all fears and phobias.

Pyrite. A very positive stone to be used when you're feeling less
than adequate. Place a piece on your desk or in your work area
and you'll soon notice a change of energy. Ideas will flow and
diplomacy will become so much easier. Your mental activity is
accelerated and accentuated. Iron Pyrite is said to increase the
oxygen supply to the blood and aid the circulatory system. It
inspires courage and confidence. When worn around the neck,
it is said to shield the wearer from negative energy and protect
the physical, etheric and emotional bodies. It aids the memory
and has also been used in healing the bone structure, the cell
composition and internal infections. Disorders of the lungs,
bronchitis and asthma are always improved by working with
Pyrite.

Quartz – Clear Crystal. The true 'energiser' crystal. Its clarity and simplicity are the keys to it's power. It raises the vibration of the user and opens up the channels for healing and communication. When cloudy, it is believed to be a doorway to the mysteries – when clear it is the power of Mother Earth herself. With Clear Quartz Crystal on or near you – you will experience an uplift of spiritual energy that imbues you with added strength and insight. As a healing crystal it works on all the chakras – balancing, clearing and energising. Clear Quartz Crystal can be programmed and reprogrammed, and has long been associated with mystics and magicians. Minerals remind me of the 'elemental' powers in their solidity and bulk they appear unchanging and permanent. However, the real magic in them is that it is all an illusion and really they are constantly changing and evolving. Clear Quartz Crystal has a slow steady pulse in tune with the beat of Mother Earth and those sensitive enough to attune can access the libraries within them. They all have a memory, some greater than others.

Record keeper Quartz Crystal is recognised by a small raised triangle or triangles located on one or more of it's faces. These are said to have been placed there by beings before our time or, more accurately, beings of the 'First Time'. Only those pure in word, thought and deed can access this knowledge and wisdom for the spiritual good of mankind. The wisdom contained therein is sealed by the triangle which acts as a portal to other dimensions and no human being of our time can alter the programming of the crystal from this dimension. Thus the secrets are safe and beyond contamination.

Rhodochrosite. This mineral is known to bring suppressed, unwanted feelings to the surface so they can be dealt with through emotional release. It helps the release of pent-up energy – transmuted into tears or anger. Either way, it is better out than in. It is symbolic of the umbilical cord and the rebirthing process. Rhodochrosite has the ability to bring events in our life, that have caused pain, to the front to so we can acknowledge them for what they are and place them in context. It proves to us that there are no coincidences and everything happens for a purpose. Each event in our life is a learning process. Some of us learn the lesson first time – while others continue to repeat the same mistakes. Working with this stone leaves you nowhere to go – except to face the truth. It makes no excuses for others and no apologies either. However, if this stone comes into your possession or if you're drawn to it, somewhere deep amongst your subconscious lies a strong desire to find the courage and power to confront an issue and move on. The opposite can also be true, those who adamantly dislike this mineral may be afraid to face something, preferring to keep it buried. Rhodochrosite aids with emotional stress, spleen, heart, circulatory system and kidneys.

Rhodonite. The stone that restores the physical energy depleted by trauma or shock. It works on the heart and solar plexus chakras, steadying and calming by grounding 'static' electricity. It helps our reserve and maintains our self-esteem when under pressure. It has been used to strengthen the inner ear and generally improve hearing. It is often used in the treatment of emphysema along with Labradorite. This stone does not always do well with other minerals and has even been known to physically move away from them. The energy seems to abhor static electricity and if placed on the top of the television it is common for the mineral to jump off.

Rose Quartz. The 'inner peace' stone – Rose Quartz is widely believed to emit a calming, cooling energy that works on all the chakras to gently remove negativity and reinstate the calm, gentle force of self-love. It restores tranquillity and clarity after times of chaos or crisis. Rose Quartz opens the crown and brow chakras producing a gentleness from within and around the user. It can restore peace and understanding to a relationship or friendship. Rose Quartz has been used to remove impurities and excess fluids from the body. It is also believed by some to soften the complexion and reduce wrinkles. Despite its name, Rose Quartz has more in common with Calcite than the Quartz family. It grows in masses, as opposed to the usual six sided points of Quartz, and large pieces are often used in places of healing and meditation rooms. It is an excellent healer of the 'first wound' which helps us to come to terms with the underlying cause. However, it does it in a gentle calming way which attunes to one's own pace.

Ruby. Known as the 'stone of nobility', the Ruby is widely believed to gather and amplify energies whilst promoting and stimulating mental concentration. It can improve your success in controversies or disputes while discouraging violence. An excellent 'shielding' stone, Ruby protects on all levels and safeguards the subconscious from psychic attack. The energy brings a recognition as to whether one needs to experience anguish or distress. Becoming aware of this helps our spiritual progression and leads us to eliminate negatives from our path. Ruby works on the lymph glands decreasing the time it takes for toxin to work through the body. Often found in jewellery and worn on the brow in Eastern countries – this, we now realise, stimulates the pineal gland which is a vital centre for all round good health. It also improves mental agility. It is said that the Ruby will lighten the darkness of one's life. Some believe that as long as you retain a Ruby, wealth will never leave you. The energy of Ruby relates to the energy of the zodiac sign Aries and the element of fire.

Ruby in Zoisite. Also known as Anyolite. This mineral stimulates the heart chakra and helps disorders relating to the flow of blood through the ventricles. It transmutes the energy of 'self' into the energy of 'group'. It is the bringer of spiritual wisdom, health, knowledge and wealth. Known as a magical crystal, some believe it can be used to facilitate access to the teachings of Merlin himself. It can create altered states of consciousness, utilising and amplifying the abilities of the mind. It promotes dreaming and stimulates the connection with, and transfer of information from, our spiritual guides. In addition, it allows the amplification of one's entire energy field. Often used in regression work and past-life recall, Ruby in Zoisite allows us to 'slip behind the veil' and retrieve information from soul memory. Hold some when you're meditating or during circle work to connect to this elusive energy flow that is usually just beyond reach. Carry a piece of Ruby in Zoisite in your purse and you will never want for money.

Rutile. It is usually found in Clear Quartz or Smoky Quartz and is seen as the fine angel hair that streaks the Quartz. This beautiful addition to Quartz opens the aura and allows universal love to flow in. It eases the transitions in our life and helps us to visualise the next step along the path. When healing with Rutile, you should stroke it through the aura, slightly above the body, in a sweeping motion away from the body. Then shake the crystal well to remove any adverse energy. This motion should be like combing the entire energy field around the body. From the heart chakra down, stroke outwards towards the ground. From the heart chakra up, stroke outwards and upward towards the sky. After the healing put the crystal down and, with your hands outstretched, run them like a big wave around the body from the ground upward. This just finishes the healing by smoothing the energies around the person receiving the healing.

They may feel this in the form of a shiver and it can leave them feeling a little emotional. Once the aura is open you can begin to work on the areas you have identified as in the most need of healing. Using Rutilated Quartz with the configurations for awakening the Kundalini fire would be powerful medicine, but not recommended for those who are of nervous disposition.

Sapphire. The 'wisdom' stone, it assists healing in all parts of the body. It especially stimulates the throat chakra and helps higher-self communication. It is widely believed that Blue Sapphire activates our primordial memory of ancient knowledge from the records related to the development of all civilisation, as well as the intuitive, psychic and astral selves. Blue Sapphire is said to have been implanted upon the Earth by kind and generous ancient 'Earth keepers' in order to assist our understanding and compassion by the energy transfers necessary for Earth healing. It aligns the chakras and releases energy blockages which restrain us from our spiritual path. It can transmute negative energies and is widely used in shamanic ceremonies for this purpose. When using it in configuration healings, hold the Sapphire over the patient, who should be lying down on the floor or couch. Make a full circle over the chakras. Start at the sacral chakra and circle upwards to the throat chakra and back down to the sacral. Do this a number of times whilst channelling peacefully. This will bring up physical creation and transmute it into artistic creativity. It can be a powerful healing for those struggling to express themselves in a materialistic world where huge competition can play havoc on anyone who is remotely sensitive.

Selenite. A member of the Gypsum family. It is the colourless, transparent variety. Sometimes formed in 'fish tails' which are particularly spectacular to behold and marvel at. It is believed that in this form it is one of the most powerful healing stones used. Selenite calms the overexcited, clears the mind gently of troubles and instils peace. Kept near you, it reduces wrinkles and tension of the brow. It stabilises one's emotions and opens the door to past-life memories which enable us to take stock of our situations – if only to reassure us that we are not repeating the same lesson. For example: If we spend one lifetime coming to terms with, say, the lesson of self-worth – and then we reincarnate without ever really coming to terms with the lesson, then the lesson is repeated. The lesson becomes harder each time until the spirit truly understands. This is the difference between accepting and really 'knowing'.

Satin Spar – has a fine grain and lustre – sometimes with a pearly, powdery finish. Some harder forms of this are known as Alabaster. If you take a sharp knife to it, like a chisel, a glassy smooth face can be achieved. This form of Selenite is useful during pregnancy when the emotions run high. It is a good balancer and teaches patience. It also calms during breastfeeding and is therefore welcome in any nursery area.

Desert Rose – is Gypsum that has been deposited, in solid form, from a solution of evaporating sea water with other minerals. It forms into hard looking round disk formations that appear like crystallised sand. If you should find yourself attracted to this mineral, it comes as a messenger to show you that you've become stuck within a programme of your own making. Therefore the simplest solution to your problem – is to dissolve the programme.

Gypsum – This interesting mineral sometimes comes looking like soft, fluffy, pale green clouds. This occurs in smaller amounts in volcanic areas where sulphuric acid fumes have reacted with limestone. In this form it is often found around beauty therapy salons because it certainly makes us feel good about ourselves. It brings together all the facets that make up a personality to work toward our highest good. It has the ability to set in motion the reversal of the ageing process on the bones and elasticity of the skin. There are other forms of Gypsum that crystallise in a variety of masses and a full range of colours. All are excellent healing tools which, in general, act on the crown or third eye chakras aligning them with the heart.

Silver. The mineral of 'new beginnings'. Malleable, magical and emotional. It allows us to accept our emotions as genuine, intuitive messages of the truth. There are exactly as many new beginnings as are required for each soul journey, as many new pages as need be turned. All we have to do is accept that we have 'screwed up' and ask for help. The problem usually lies in the difficulty we have in accepting that we are wrong or have made a mistake or that we've taken the wrong path. So we continue – locked into a pattern. Silver is a mirror of the soul. It guides us on our path and teaches patience in the understanding of our chosen tasks. Silver gently increases our ability to comprehend a lesson learnt. It is a gentle but strong emotional balancer and enhances communication. It is most associated with the Moon goddess and worn by those 'Moon based' in their workings (sometimes known as 'Moon blessed'). The children of the Moon are individuals who follow their emotions. They are moveable, changeable, creative and are in harmony with the great Earth Mother. They are opposite to the children of the Sun, who are in harmony with Father Sky and attracted to the solar disc, or the golden orb, Gold.

Smoky Quartz. The 'dark Crystal'. Smoky Quartz is widely believed to promote calm and inner understanding. It releases old negativities, helping us to let go of resentment, anger, fear and guilt. It helps with exploration of the inner self by penetrating the darkness with light and love. It is an excellent meditation stone, being mildly sedative, and can enhance dreams and channelling abilities. Lie down and close your eyes – check your breathing pattern and relax. Place a piece of Smoky Quartz on your forehead. Allow your consciousness to be consumed by this cool crystal. As you travel deep into the crystal try not to think or hold onto any individual thoughts. Slowly a new sense of awareness will become apparent. A highly secretive, occult and definitely mystical sense. One of travelling interdimensionally and exploring other realms. Recapturing the memories of past lives, travelling through time and space, delving into the memory of the crystal itself. Learning the knowledge and wisdom that has been locked there, deep within its matrix. Find your way around the inner crystal chambers until you feel quite sure of your whereabouts. Look for the chamber with a golden hue about it. Feel yourself being pulled into this chamber. It is the chamber that heals all ills, physical, emotional or spiritual. Here you can make your request for healing – but take care to ask only of your needs. You will be given only the karmic healing that you need – and, most importantly, that you have worked to deserve. Smoky Quartz, treated with respect by the many, is accessible to all who approach with sincerity and trust. Smoky Quartz energy aligns with the zodiac sign Capricorn and, likewise, is earthy and grounded with hidden qualities.

Sodalite. Sodalite eliminates confusion, enabling us to find our 'truth' in all situations and weight it against the truth of others. It acts on the brow and throat chakras with a slow, pulsing energy that calms and clarifies. It also helps us to recognise and deal with rigid thought patterns that lurk within our nature. Sodalite helps with phobias and calms panic attacks. Essentially, it has a reassuring and calming effect on our instincts. It is a good stone for the oversensitive and defensive personality types. It is a great help in group work. It provides a platform of trust, fellowship and solidarity that unites the aims and goals of the whole group. It allows the universal laws to filter into our mind and body in a stimulating yet understandable way – without the hard work! Sodalite is known to work on the pineal gland and has a direct effect on the metabolism. It also is believed to strengthen the blood and lymphatic system. This mineral, used in conjunction with aromatherapy, has had encouraging results on the lymphatic system. Sodalite is used to prevent insomnia and treat disorders associated with calcium deficiencies. It is sometimes associated with the zodiac sign Sagittarius especially in the colour range light red, yellow and lavender blue.

Stichtite. This mineral should be held and meditated with. It clears blockages which then seep into the system and are carried through the body to be expelled. For example – a severe backache problem. Meditating on the backache and asking the mineral to take the pain away will trigger self-healing. The body expels the damaged cells which, for a while, may mean some mild discomfort usually in the form of sickness or diarrhoea. The process of helping those with weight problems is extremely similar, particularly during the period when the metabolism is readjusting itself. You should always wash Stichtite carefully after a healing or meditation. Its ability to retain the bad energy is weak and has been known to 'give it back to you'. It can be very useful in pregnancy and for water retention as it protects and aids the skin in returning to its former condition. I have been aware of healers using it on hyperactive children to calm them down and stop erratic behaviour problems. However, the conclusions so far have led me to believe that the best results have been achieved when treating the whole family. Usually the behaviour has a direct relationship with problems amongst the adults or other family members which the sensitive child externalises.

Sugilite. The great questions of 'Who am I? Why am I here? Where am I going?' are all summarised within this stone. The realisation that we are allowed to question flows from this mineral. It is often worn as a sign of respect for the unknowable especially the dark, purple coloured variety. There is false Sugilite on the market, mainly inlaid in fine jewellery so be wary. This is quite a 'new' find and, as yet, little experience of its healing properties has been documented. Healers agree that this mineral offers relief for headaches and has the ability to absorb and transform negative energies.

Sulphur. An attraction to sulphur is usually a cry for help, in so much as 'like attracts like'. It assists in identifying and removing negative, wilful traits in our nature that can affect thought processing. For example, if a ticket is written and placed near a piece of sulphur saying 'Please do not touch', although it is there to prevent anyone ending up with smelly fingers or the sulphur crumbling, there are those amongst us that are compelled to touch. This is the element that sulphur deals with. The bright, yellow, 'unreal' colour and the crumbly texture send a signal which is hard to resist. However, once we have touched it, our skin is coated in an awful odour which is hard to remove – just like negative traits. It is sometimes used as a natural fumigant and can also work well as an insect repellent. When crushed, it can be added to a bath to ease and reduce swelling in painful joints. Placed on growths and tumours it is believed that Sulphur has the ability to absorb the negative cells. All the patient has to do is realise that they need healing and ask for it. After the healing the Sulphur should be buried in the earth. I have noted that Sulphur, used during a meditation, raises the vibration in the entire room and those struggling to open up latent psychic abilities are able to use this energy. A number of colour therapists use the energy of sulphur for the same reason.

Sunstone. Sometimes referred to as 'Burnt Moonstone', Sunstone is the positive energy in this type of feldspar. It sparkles due to the Hematite or Goethite content and is generally used to energise and clear the chakras. It makes the chakras radiate warmth like sunshine on a summer's day. The feeling soon spreads, relieving pressure and pain. Sunstone represents the solar disc bringing the life force of the universe and good fortune with it. Wear it around your neck to clear the throat chakra, increase fertility and protect the physical and spiritual bodies. It is a good antidepressant especially during the winter months.

Tektite. Tektite is a generic name for the substance formed by a piece of rock falling through the atmosphere. Atmospheric friction generates intense heat and on, impact with the Earth, a molten 'glass' is formed that cools into a hard, semi-translucent material. There is much active discussion as to whether such impacts are caused by meteor fragments or simply by pieces of terrestrial minerals that have been thrown high into the atmosphere by such events as volcanic explosion. Personally, I tend towards the view that both are possible and, therefore, treat each piece I find on its own merits. Moldavite is one of the best known examples of a Tektite and originates in a specific site in the western area of the Czech Republic. Because of the fact that meteorites or comets come from other worlds and that an impact is required to create the melting of terrestrial rock, healers believe that Tektites are not only a link to other worlds, but also to creation itself and the union of energy and matter. Tektites act to balance the masculine and feminine properties of our character and stimulate spiritual growth. They are believed

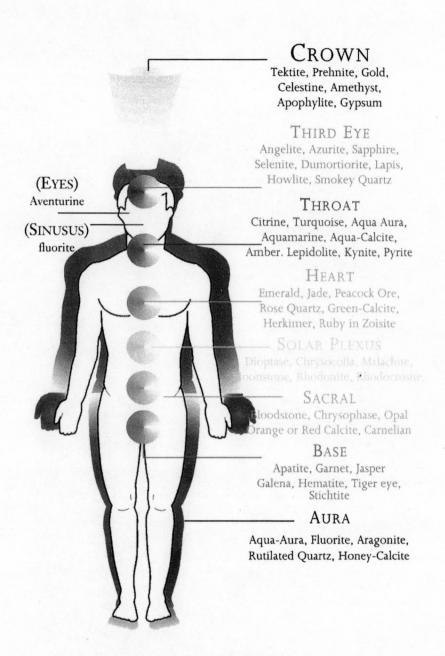

CROWN
Tektite, Prehnite, Gold,
Celestine, Amethyst,
Apophylite, Gypsum

THIRD EYE
Angelite, Azurite, Sapphire,
Selenite, Dumortiorite, Lapis,
Howlite, Smokey Quartz

(EYES)
Aventurine

(SINUSUS)
fluorite

THROAT
Citrine, Turquoise, Aqua Aura,
Aquamarine, Aqua-Calcite,
Amber. Lepidolite, Kynite, Pyrite

HEART
Emerald, Jade, Peacock Ore,
Rose Quartz, Green-Calcite,
Herkimer, Ruby in Zoisite

SOLAR PLEXUS
Dioptase, Chrysocolla, Malachite,
Moonstone, Rhodozite, Rhodocrosite,

SACRAL
Bloodstone, Chrysophase, Opal
Orange or Red Calcite, Carnelian

BASE
Apatite, Garnet, Jasper
Galena, Hematite, Tiger eye,
Stichtite

AURA
Aqua-Aura, Fluorite, Aragonite,
Rutilated Quartz, Honey-Calcite

Figure 1   The chakras of the body –
and the most common crystals relating to it

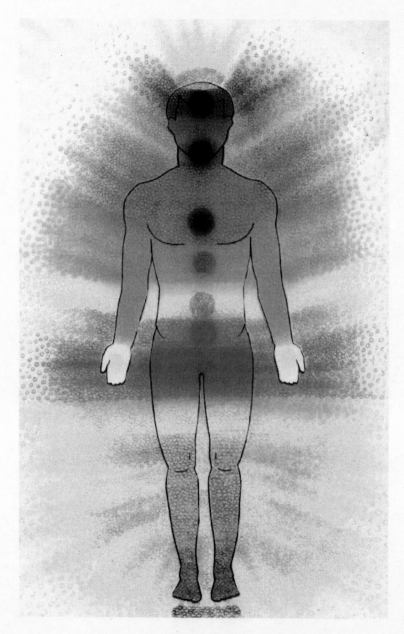

Figure 2   The normal, healthy aura

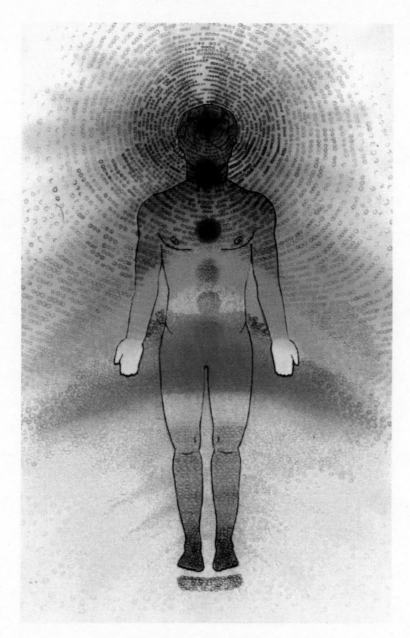

Figure 3   The aura – under stress attack

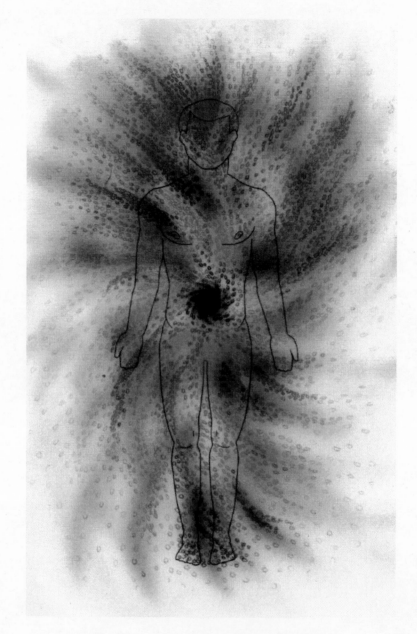

Figure 4   The aura – under violent attack

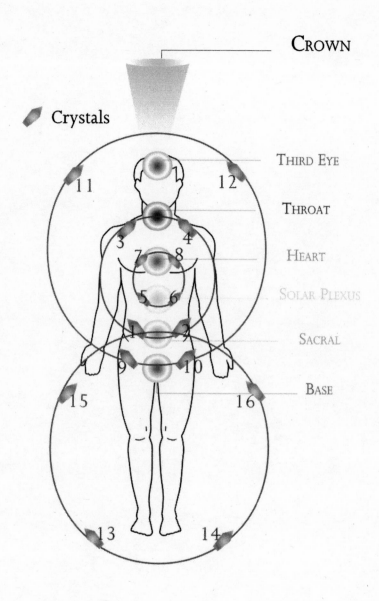

CROWN

Crystals

THIRD EYE

THROAT

HEART

SOLAR PLEXUS

SACRAL

BASE

Figure 5   The 'Vesica Piscis' configuration

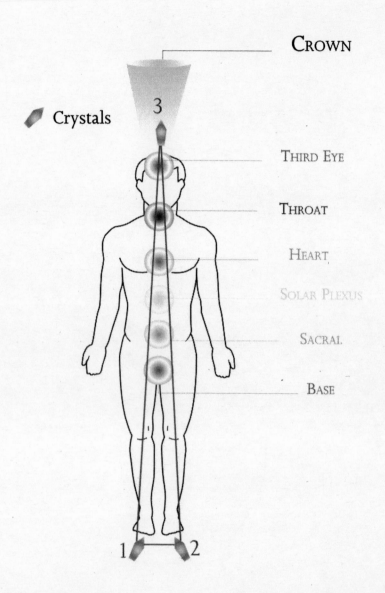

CROWN

Crystals

THIRD EYE

THROAT

HEART

SOLAR PLEXUS

SACRAL

BASE

Figure 6   The Triangulation configuration

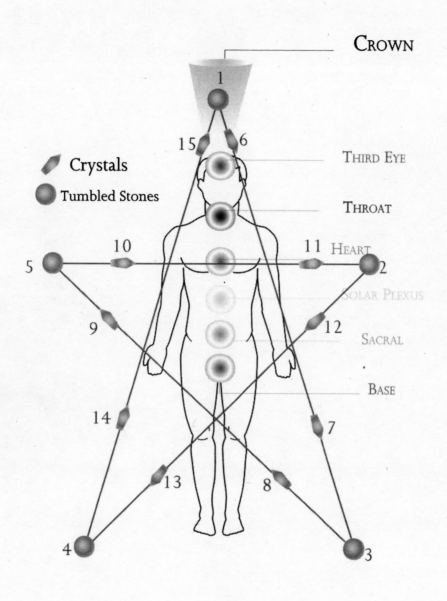

CROWN

Crystals

Tumbled Stones

THIRD EYE

THROAT

HEART

SOLAR PLEXUS

SACRAL

BASE

Figure 7   The Pentagram configuration

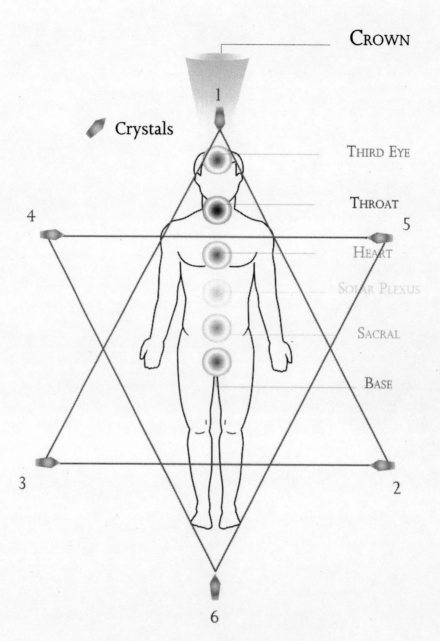

CROWN

Crystals

THIRD EYE

THROAT

HEART

SOLAR PLEXUS

SACRAL

BASE

Figure 8   The 'Star of David' configuration

to open channels through which inner knowledge and under-standing can flow. Tektites assist in the gathering and retention of spiritual knowledge and greatly facilitate spiritual communi-cation. They also protect the knowledge you have already gathered and prevent its loss. Often used in healing on the chakras to balance, and even reverse, the direction of energy output. Tektites are often worn as talisman and believed to aid fertility and growth.

Tiger Eye is a member of the Quartz family and usually found in South Africa. It works on balancing the energy of the lower chakras – base, sacral and solar plexus – as well as stimulating the kundalini energy. Tiger Eye can be found in a variety of colours and a mix of them, carried in your pocket and tumbled between the fingers during times of stress, has a distinctive calming effect.

Gold Tiger Eye is useful when you're feeling complacent but, in reality, you should be more grounded and paying attention to detail. It grounds the body allowing the reason, rather than emotion, to trigger the patterns of thought. It is very good during school exams or business meetings.

Red Tiger Eye is useful when you're lethargic and need motivation. It can help to speed up a slow metabolism, and stimulate sexual interest for those with a low sex drive.

Blue Tiger Eye works in an opposite way to Red. It calms the overanxious, the quick tempered and people who are phobic. It also eases the stress from times when you simply feel 'hot and bothered'. It appears to slow the metabolism and the lower energy centres. It cools the overactive sex drive and sexual frustrations.

Topaz. Renowned the world over for its healing properties, Topaz is found in jewellery of all shapes and sizes – though probably best in rings. Blue Topaz, in particular, helps the brow and throat chakras. It is widely used in meditation and offers a direct route to the 'higher' self. It holds a special attraction for the water signs of the zodiac (Blue for Aquarians and Piscians – Red/Yellow for Scorpians). It balances the emotions and is often given as a token of love. Golden Yellow Topaz is often used in the rejuvenation of cellular structures and to strengthen the solar plexus.

Tourmaline. A powerful ally in the healing of mental disorders. It is able to assist the troubled mind and dispel negative thought patterns. It destroys the build up of illusionary paranoia and strengthens the will. It is very useful for sufferers of dyslexia by stimulating the brain and helping hand-to-eye co-ordination, assimilation and movement. The colour ranges, from pink to green and black, are good for balancing the polarities of all the chakras. It can also be found in reds, yellows and browns, but these have a different quality. Noticeably, people who are drawn to this colour range are often having difficulty with their sexuality. For people who work with tree and plant magic, Tourmaline aligns to the 'divas' within nature and, when you bury a little in the garden flower beds, your blooms will benefit tremendously. It is widely believed that, when Tourmaline is offered to the 'tree spirits', your wishes will be answered and, if asked to keep the insects at bay in the vegetable plot, your crop will remain untouched. In fact – Tourmaline loves being in the garden. For a good healing, place a circle of Tourmaline around you in your garden and channel positive energy from source into your body. Then direct it to the area required. It will amplify the healing threefold and the Earth will take away all the negative debris.

Tourmalinated Lepidolite. Believed to be a very powerful combination of Lepidolite, 'the stone of transition', striated with Tourmaline, 'the teller stone'. Lepidolite helps with the smooth transition of energies from the less spiritual to those of universal light, hope and acceptance – leading to a new level of self-awareness – whilst Tourmaline imbues it with enhanced healing powers and protection. It is used for those suffering from addictions and brings awareness of their cause, high-lighting the denial and bringing acceptance of their existence. It then helps in taking the steps towards living without crutches.

Turquoise. The 'profound master healer', Turquoise is widely believed to help in the absorption of all nutrients, strengthening the entire anatomy. It aids tissue regeneration and is a powerful protector against all environmental pollutants. Turquoise relates, in particular, to the throat chakra. It enhances creative expression, peace of mind and emotional balance. It promotes communication with both the physical and spiritual worlds and strengthens friendship and loyalty. Amongst healers it is widely accepted that Turquoise has exceptional powers of psychic protection and, therefore, should never be handled by anyone but the owner – no matter how close they may be! Many native American tribes celebrate Turquoise as the 'reflection' of Father Sky and wear elaborate pieces of jewellery inlaid with the pale blue stone to protect them during the night time when the sky is dark or at times when, during sacred ceremonies, their spirit roams free as their body rests and waits for them inside the 'kiva' or 'sweat lodge'.

Ulexite is usually recognisable by its more popular name of 'TV stone' due to its clarity. Its texture is soft, like Gypsum, and forms naturally in rounded masses like puff balls. Although insoluble in cold water it becomes more soluble in hot water. It is what is known as an 'evaporative mineral', just like Gypsum which is the first mineral to be deposited in solid form from evaporating sea water. Anhydrite and Halite are also evaporative minerals but are less common in retail crystal shops. Ulexite aids one with inner vision and brings into focus that which might otherwise be too close to evaluate objectively. Because of its soft energy many women like to meditate with this mineral, benefiting from its properties of skin rejuvenation. It can be used on the brow chakra to enhance visual acuity and dispel negative head energy. This mineral aids transformation and becomes an ally when dealing with unwanted change.

Unakite is pink feldspar, green epidote and Quartz together. It is more usually found as a tumbled stone from the Jasper family. It works as a grounding crystal and acts on the root cause of an illness allowing you to identify underlying problems and the cause of an imbalance. It aids growth of skin tissue, hair and weight. It is very good for those convalescing after a major illness or operation. Unakite has an extremely feminine energy – gentle and passive. Try keeping some tumbled stones in your pocket or in a small dish at home. You'll soon find an air of calm that enables you to ground those niggling issues before they can grow into major problems. Unakite is often placed on TV sets to dissipate the EMF energies from the apparatus – but, then again, I have heard reports of such TVs breaking down. It appears that the stones have the ability to turn the EMFs in on themselves and shorting the circuits.

5

Symptoms and diagnosis

Diagnosis is probably the most important stage in crystal healing, but I do think that I should fully explain my approach and the significance I attach to the careful diagnosing of the subject or patient. I believe that an effective diagnosis has to consider two aspects of the symptoms being presented. Firstly, there is the more obvious aspect of the outward symptom itself, and secondly there is the underlying cause.

Now, so that there is no misunderstanding here, I am a firm believer in the abilities of the medical profession. I have never endorsed the school of thought that attempts to replace conventional medicine with alternative healing. But I do believe that the two approaches have a great deal to offer in support of each other – a belief that has been endorsed by many medical practitioners over the years. The medical diagnosis is principally aimed at the outward symptom and, in the pressures of today's practice, most doctors have little time to pursue the underlying cause. This does not mean that they don't care by a long way. It simply means that there is a role for responsible 'alternative' practitioners (and I can't tell you how much I hate that term) who are prepared to take the time to help uncover these under-lying issues and help prevent further manifestations of triggered illnesses. In short, though there are many of the medical establishment who still 'pooh-pooh' all other forms of healing than their own, there is definitely a growing support for our work from the very midst of traditional medicine. For myself, I prefer to support the work of the doctor wherever possible – and those who are still too prejudiced to allow us any credibility are, in my opinion, cutting themselves and their patients off from another possibility for cure. It seems that, in life, we sometimes have to travel an awfully long way – only to discover *how much we don't know*.

What has baffled many in coming to terms with the energy of crystal healing is 'How can it possibly work?' and 'Is it possible for one to intuitively find the correct crystals or minerals for themselves?' Well, crystal healing can and does receive an incredible rate of success and improvement in health for the patients who choose to try alternative healing. My experience in the past has been that, although it is largely unappreciated and undervalued by 'the establishment', it is very often these same people who, under circumstances beyond their control medically have proved to have the greatest results with crystal healing. Perhaps we have to be put in that position primarily in order to fail to resist. Once the barriers are down we 'naturally' become more sensitised and maybe that is all it takes. We become more connected and find 'our' way.

The main aim, at the first session with a new patient, is to diagnose not only the symptoms exhibited but also their under-lying cause or causes. This may seem fairly obvious, but it is often not as simple as it seems. The healer must learn to listen with both their physical and 'inner' ears. In other words – you must always look for the real chain of events that has led them to your door. One illustration of this, that I have seen so many times, is a patient who comes to you complaining of back pains and general stiffness in their neck and shoulders. Now you should never overlook the physical (perhaps they have been involved in a car accident or some similar trauma), but if they tell you that their pain has come on gradually, you should look for signs of stress in their lifestyle. This is a typical 'domino' effect diagnosis.

Picture this scenario: The patient has come under increased pressure at work – perhaps they have reached middle-age and feel threatened by younger competitors for their job. They take this pressure home and their spouse and family have noticed a withdrawal in their behaviour and start to apply more pressure – cajoling them to return to 'normal'. They are now under pressure from both of their main areas of life. This has made them tense and, as we all know, the first place that tension manifests itself is in the neck and shoulders. They are now walking around with permanently tense shoulder and neck muscles. Their shoulders have become rounded – looking as if *they're carrying the weight of the world*. The shoulder and neck muscle groups become overtired from this constant tension and their spine has begun taking on the strain. So, by the time this patient arrives at your door, they are complaining of back pain. Your diagnosis, therefore, has to not only address their immediate problem, the pain and discomfort, but must also deal with the root cause – their own self-image and insecurity. The healing process will be started by you and your crystals, but it has to be completed by the patient themselves.

There are many crystal healers who say to me 'I'm a healer – not a counsellor'. I strongly disagree. Those of us who enter the world of alternative healing have to use our best endeavours to supplement the efforts of the medical profession. The big difference is that we approach the patient in a more holistic way. Our aim is not to perform open-heart surgery or to mend broken bones – but to restore our patients to a state of overall 'wellness'. Talking to your patient – and listening carefully to what they're telling you – is probably the most valuable part of the healing diagnosis. You should learn to pay careful attention not only to what they say – but also to what they don't say. The natural sensitivity, that all healers work hard to develop, is arguably their greatest gift. This sensitivity should begin with the first consultation and guide you through the course of healing. Your intuition is a valuable tool in diagnosis – you should listen to what it tells you.

The first healing session

The first session is always the most important, setting the tempo for the entire healing relationship. Talking, listening and understanding what you hear are all critical at this point. Remember that every healer has their own special way of working. However, with over twenty years working with crystal energy this is what I find works for me.

I take the patient into the healing room and try to reassure them that they are safe and should feel relaxed and comfortable.

Any reservations they might have usually emerge at this point and it may not surprise you to know that I can learn as much about the physical condition of the patient from these first few moments as from the rest of the healing put together.

Once seated I need them to feel comfortable so they can open up. At this point I'm not trying to uncover their entire life history. What I require most for a successful healing is for them to simply relax and allow their chakras to begin to open. When we warm to someone we naturally open up relax and become less tense, that in itself is part of the healing process. Once the aura is prized even slightly open the body's natural survival process will kick in and automatically send out a kind of 'distress signal' to *source* for aid. Like a battery being connected for a recharge.

The healthy aura is bright and vibrant. It radiates from the physical body, visible for several feet – sometimes even further. The aura of someone in pain or under stress extends no more than a few inches and, in severe cases or in times of grief, even less than that. What is actually happening is a 'closing down' or self-protection program. As the patient under emotional stress tries to stop the pain they pull in the auric field tight around the body. It has the desired effect of shutting out the world so that nothing or no one can hurt them. Unfortunately it also can cut them off from their spiritual bodies and the great energy source. The issue in any form of spiritual healing is to reconnect the vital life force to source and, to enable that to happen, you need the patient to consciously warm to you and naturally start to open up. This will make the healing process much simpler and speedier. We all have an inbuilt self-healing program. Unfortunately, under certain conditions, we get out of balance and, particularly if we're suffering from low self-esteem or start to feel that life is not worth living, we can go into *self-destruct*.

This raises another issue. Even if someone resists all forms of help, even after asking or coming to a healing session, I have been amazed how often a complete change takes place within their aura and how, more often then not, by the end of the healing session the healing process has began. But, if someone is determined to harm themselves and their only reason for attending the healing centre is to make others feel bad or take pity on them, that is their karma. I refuse to be put in a position of taking on another's karma and, though I will give all the help I possibly can, at the end of the day that is their choice.

If the patient is in a comfortable sitting position the healing is structured around them. If they are more comfortable lying down then a move to the couch is taken and a light cover is placed over them. The initial work is done by passing the hands slowly over the body; this allows the healer to feel the energy centres and structure of the aura. Then a selection of crystals are used within the auric field, some are pulled through the aura while others are placed on the physical body. After the healing the patient is given a chance to select a crystal they feel drawn to and given the opportunity to ask questions about their healing, diagnosis and the healing regime. The prognosis consists of two things, one is the course of the healing treatment and the way in which the healer recommends the treatment continues and the other part of the regime is how they can expect to feel and the way it will affect them.

Remember, as we have already discussed, the aim of healing is to induce a situation whereby the individual can heal themselves. Therefore, the greatest help a healer can offer is to help that individual gain some degree of control. To give them something constructive to be part of and, of course, the one thing that everyone can be their very best at is being themselves.

The choice of which particular crystal to use for a specific complaint will vary greatly, depending on a number of factors. Not the least of these is the healer's own experience. As you spend more time working with the crystals you will find yourself being drawn or 'guided' to try different combinations. The most important thing to remember is that we are all individuals and we each have a unique link to the source energy. Because of this individuality you will find subtle differences between your experiences and those of other healers. For this reason – I offer the following chapter only as a guide to the most common ailments and the crystals I have found to be most effective in healing them. I would strongly advise that you make your own chart and fill in any new or different crystal combinations that you find working well for you.

6

Ailments
and
crystals

Aches and pains

Fluorite. Use to smooth over the painful area like a small iron stroking in the direction of the heart. Cleanse in cold water frequently.

Spotted Jasper. Hold in the leading hand, loosely in the palm. Become aware of your breathing and concentrate on inhaling positive light energy to the count of eight, then exhale negative energy from where the ache or pain is to the count of nine. Every breath will seem to take away a little more of the pain. Soon you will feel the pulse of the stone in the palm of your hand and you will realise the pain has gone.

Addictions

Dioptase. This beautiful green stone acts like a conductor of energy activating the nerve endings and the sending and receiving of messages around the body. It helps addictions by 'emotionally' adjusting these signals from 'I must have', 'I need', 'I can't', to 'I'm OK, my energy is balanced'. Keep it near you at all times, it becomes a comfort stone, and it works.

Lepidolite. The Mica Lepidolite brings clarity to all things and, by working with it, all addictions are put in prospective over time. With that comes the will to drop the negatives one holds onto and swap them for positive thoughts which bring peace. Meditate with it and hold it when the going gets tough.

Alcoholism

Hematite. Keep in your pocket or wear around your neck as a pendent. Every time you feel tempted, reach for this cool silver grey stone; it will act as your conscience and alert your psyche to be on guard.

Anger

White Howlite. Use to dispel powerful build ups of negative energy. At this point the one most likely to be affected is yourself through stress – migraines etc. Whilst holding this stone learn to breath through the anger and, in time, self-control will follow.

Peridot. This soothing gemstone discreetly works away at dispelling the energy build up that causes anger. Wear it as a piece of jewellery or keep it in your pocket at all times. It is difficult to be angry when holding a piece of Peridot.

Anorexia

Rose Quartz. This stone teaches one to love themselves and if you love, you care. To care about someone you would always want the best for them and so look after them. Pick a lovely smooth tumbled piece of Rose Quartz and gently stroke it over the body. It emits a strong love energy, it feels good. It makes one see beauty in all things and works at the very root of anorexia. Use as an energiser for water and leave a piece in your drinking glass.

Stichtite. Works on the kundalini stimulating movement and cleansing. It allows us to 'cream off' the *real* reasons for why we feel and act as we do. It helps us to face the very issues that we perceive as 'demons' – which are often of our own making. In other words, it shifts our concepts and perceptions. It has some success with anorexia because it shifts the thoughts from self and slow, low energy to a faster vibration leaving little time to contemplate. Meditate with this mineral and sleep with it.

Arthritis

Carnelian and or Fluorite. Take a smooth piece of Carnelian or Fluorite and smooth it over the body, stroking towards the heart. When the stone becomes warm, wash in cold water. Fluorite is especially good at absorbing the heat from throbbing limbs.

Azurite. This beautiful blue mineral has a vibration that is absorbed into skin tissues and works its way into the body. Keep in the area most used for relaxing, the bedroom or lounge, and hold to meditate with. Worn as jewellery and kept close to the skin.

Chrysocolla. Use in items of jewellery to wear close to the skin for the body to absorb the energy. Works on strengthening the muscular structure and joints. Chrysocolla brings balance and breaks down the pressure that gathers in weak areas of the body relieving the stress. It calms the base, navel and heart chakras eliminating negative energies. A good mineral to keep around.

Asthma

Amber. This fossilised tree resin has an electrical property that emits a vibration subtle enough to stimulate the throat chakra to defend itself from infections, nasal catarrh, asthma and hay fever. Worn on the throat chakra as a pendant or amulet.

Aura

Rutilated Quartz. The aura is a delicate area, usually first affected in cases of illness and shock. Rutilated Quartz has an energy naturally suited to the aura and working with it is extremely successful especially in cases of tight auras that do not allow enough life force in to replenish that which is used. Usually found in Clear Quartz or Smoky Quartz the fine angel hair that streaks the Quartz is Rutile. This beautiful Quartz opens the aura and allows universal love to flow in. It eases the transitions in one's life and helps one visualise the next step along the path. When healing with Rutile, stroke it through the aura slightly above the body in a sweeping motion away from the body. Then shake the crystal to move the energy. This motion should be like combing the entire energy field around the body. From the heart chakra down stroke outwards towards the ground. From the heart chakra upward stroke outwards and upward towards the sky. Wash the crystal after use. Those sensitive enough to feel the vibration will notice a tingling sensation all around the body.

Autism

Ametrine. A terrific stimulant. I have had success with children allowing them to explore a bowl full of assorted tumbled stones. However, the Ametrine seems to cause the most excitement. Can be worn as a pendant. Also strung into a rosary it works well for sufferers of autism of all ages. Ametrine seems to speed up the time taken to process a thought and aids communication. Care should be taken, however, with someone who is hyperactive as Ametrine can cause a little chaos and excitement.

Apatite. Again a good stimulant of 'right brain–left brain' activity. A mineral worthy of exploration. My experience has been that it has the ability to speed up slow methodical computations of the mind, promoting confidence in speech and behaviour. Without doubt an unusual mineral.

Bladder

Amber. Amber placed on the abdomen during a healing is believed to kill infections and aid the healing process. Working and meditating with Amber balances the lower chakras.

Bloodstone. Used to make elixirs and to energise water for drinking. Carry Bloodstone with you and wear as jewellery. The vibration stimulates the weakest chakras into responding and lifts the energy there.

Blood pressure

Amethyst. Calming and soothing, a good general balancer that works well for sufferers of high blood pressure. A few tumbled pieces placed in the drinking water work well, as does wrapping a piece of Amethyst in thin fabric and holding on the temples. Amethyst Geodes within the home induce a peaceful exchange of energy between family members. Wear thin long strands of Amethyst beads rather than a heavy pendant, and try sleeping with some under the pillow.

Calcium control

Dolomite. Meditate with this mineral at least once a week for any effect. You will find subconsciously your food craving change and the body readjusts.

Cancers

Opal. Meditating with Opal is a very gentle experience. It opens the mind and shifts the awareness. Try this visualisation. Using your Opal, picture your cancer as described to you by your doctor. See it in colour as a living, breathing entity. Now picture the same area of the body as it should look in its healthy state. Again ask your doctor for help with this as it is important. As you see the cancer within, visualise gradually taking away its energy and slowly it begins to shrink. Now return your thoughts to the healthy picture and give that vision life by breathing energy into it. Every day for a week work on this concept and each time drain more energy from the negative picture and give more energy to the positive picture. In the second week, work only on the positive picture seeing it as a healthy part of your body. You must give the picture life by using all your will and tell yourself it is healthy. The Opal used in this way amplifies all of your positive energy focusing it to heal.

Sulphur. The energy of this vivid yellow mineral has a huge effect on both the emotional and spiritual bodies. Use as a focus for meditation whilst working on the elimination of negative cells, to prevent them gathering in masses. Some healers have success with reducing cancerous growths by using the rapid rhythmic vibration of Sulphur around the body. Crushed Sulphur is often used in baths and as a fumigant to repel insects. Known for its sacred and magical properties, the yellow colour of Sulphur has been used in native American sand paintings as a pigment to colour the sand for many nations. Amongst the Navajo, the medicine man constructs a painting of different coloured sands, each of which relates to a different spirit. With the spirits thus summoned, the medicine man enlists their aid in performing the healing. The Navajo believe that, when summoned in this way, the spirits are bound to attend. Through a long ritual with chants, prayers and his medicine bundle, the medicine man becomes one with the spirits and shares their powers. He then sets about healing, blessing, drumming, dancing and making offerings on behalf of the patient to effect a cure. The spirits move the illness into the painting and, thus, out into the ether. At the completion of the ceremony, the medicine man destroys the painting by collecting and burying it outside the kiva, allowing Mother Earth to absorb the harmful elements and dismiss the spirits back to whence they came. This is a very simplified version of a powerful ritual that uses crushed minerals to heal through colour and vibration. However, a powerful visualisation for the Sulphur to absorb the cancer cells done with intent has been known to be very effective in reversing negative energies. Once the Sulphur is saturated take into the garden and bury or burn it. Either way is correct and it leaves the responsibility up to the elements to disperse.

Hematite. Carried or worn as a pendant (or amulet), it works by absorbing negative energies and grounding them. A good 'destresser'.

Calcite. There is a calcite for every condition and severity. Hold the calcite and allow the stone to take away your frustrations and hurt. Meditate with it and allow the Calcite to attune to you and your own personal needs.

Cellulite

Clear Quartz Crystal. Use to meditate with. Also, a tumbled crystal can be used to massage the cellulite area. Programme to speed up the metabolic rate. Use in drinking water.

Channelling

Angelite. Good for communicating with the angelic realms.

Apophyllite. Facilitates attunement to the astral dimensions and altered states of being.

Celestine. Synchronises one's spiritual and emotional bodies aiding communication from source and triggering the soul memory.

Calcite. Aqua Calcite teaches by example. It has evolved through density to clarity and shows you the way. Attune to the energies of Aqua Calcite and you can follow.

Chrohn's disease

Peridot. Wear as a necklace or pendant. This gemstone works on the nerves and stress level, calming and aiding the functions of the abdomen and solar plexus.

Circulation

Copper. Wear as a bracelet or item of jewellery. You know it's working when you turn green! Copper is useful for moving energy around, a few nuggets of Copper in the pocket works well too.

Garnet. Often worn in a ring, it is most effective in an open-back setting allowing it to touch the skin. Use to meditate with, and in healing, pass over the body towards the heart.

Hematite. This is used to ground energy and I find it works well for circulatory problems by dragging the energy down to the feet. Keep in your pocket or wear as a ring, pendant or necklace. Useful as a 'touch stone' smoothed between the fingers and thumb.

Colds

Fluorite. Excellent for sinus and congestion caused by colds and 'flu. Chose a purple to green coloured tumbled stone and rub on the temples and sinuses. Wash frequently in cold water. Keep it under the pillow.

Coma

Ametrine. Used to stimulate the activity of the brain, works on all major organs. Keep under the pillow. Experiment during the two main Moon phases. New Moon to Full Moon is usually the time of greatest activity, and Ametrine is most potent then.

Concentration

Blue Tigers Eye. A calming, soothing stone that allows one to keep on one train of thought at a time. Stops the overactive mind from wandering.

Carnelian. Use as a stone to tumble in your pocket when you feel your mind wander. Wear as a pendant.

Constipation

Red Calcite. Works on the cause of the problem which relates to a retention of body waste. Red Calcite stimulates physical energy. Keep a piece on the bedside table.

Courage

Pyrite. Wear around your neck as a pendant. Keep on your desk at work. It assists one in thinking positively and working on the here and now intensely. Therefore, there is less to worry about because you have dealt with it before it becomes a problem.

Tigers Eye. Inspires the energy of action after thought. Softens the 'bloody minded' element of one's nature and fiery temperament. Teaches composure and tactics. Use to tumble in your pocket when processing thoughts.

Rhodochrosite. You either love or hate this stone. If you hate it you recognise something about yourself you dislike and so probably should work with it as you need to address this issue. Gives one the fortitude to overcome emotional trauma. Stops denial and the 'Let's pretend that never happened' syndrome. Suddenly, self-respect takes over. Once attuned to this crystal, one starts fighting back.

Cramps

Lodestone. The 'alchemist' stone renowned for its magnetic properties. Placed at the bottom of the bed it will aid a good night's rest. Carry in your pocket during the day.

Cysts

Clear Quartz Crystal. Use to attune to during meditation and place the cyst, by visualisation, into the crystal. Do this for two weeks and then bury the crystal in the garden. An old wives' tale that has a certain amount of truth and success. I have found it may take a couple of months to remove the cysts but go they will!

Depression

Honey Calcite. Works by taking grey areas from the aura and dispersing negativity. Attunes to the solar plexus correcting polarities and imbalances. Use to hold when meditating and keep near you in the home or work place.

Carnelian. A lovely piece of tumbled Carnelian lifts a gloomy day. Used like worry beads or kept in the pocket they dispel troubles and worries. Wash daily.

Lepidolite. The wondrous colour of Lepidolite alone should shift depression. It illuminates any dark areas in one's life and lifts the energy levels. Lepidolite's vibration works on many levels and has incredible success with depression. Meditate with and place on the solar plexus during a healing.

Diabetes

Malachite. Wear as a pendant or around the waist. The vibration of Malachite stimulates the navel and solar plexus area. Use to meditate with and attune to. During a healing place on the abdomen.

Opal. Use during a healing underneath the body in the lower back area. Stimulates the pineal gland, pancreas and spleen. A powerful healer often found in jewellery.

Diarrhoea

Dog Tooth Calcite. The vibration of this Calcite works on the energy centres of the body that have been knocked out of sync. Keep on the desk or in the work place. A stubborn crystal that will slow the body down.

Digestion

Chrysocolla. The healing energy of this stone has benefited those who suffer from digestive or stomach problems. It balances the system and alleviates tensions that encroach upon this area. Use to meditate with and wear as jewellery.

Dreams

Amethyst. To bring back the wisdom of dreams, to aid the memory of astral projection. Worn as an amulet or used to sleep with.

Blue Howlite. Brings back the wisdom from dreams, allows one to access the dream state after waking. Hold when drifting off. Keep under the pillow or place in your dream catcher.

Blue Calcite. Blue Calcite is a great stone to facilitate the dream state. Hold and meditate with. Spend time with and attune to when wishing to accelerate growth of knowledge of the astral dimensions.

Drug Addictions

Hematite. This is a strong stone which many do not like, perhaps under the shiny surface lurks the opposite side of their personality. We often do not like our other side and this stone brings it out. It makes a good stone to work with when dealing with drug addictions because it makes one face the real issues.

Usually these are our failings or fears. Keep Hematite on you. Wear around your neck as a pendant or keep some in your pocket. Its energy does help.

Ears

Amber. Soothes earache. Hold and meditate with. At bedtime place under your pillow or hold in your hand as you try to drift off. Wear around the neck to dissipate negative energy.

Rhodonite. Hold and meditate with. Take two tumbled pieces and rub gently one behind each ear. Take them up wide towards the top of the ears then down close next to the back of the ears and down the neck to the shoulder. Repeat until the stones become warm and then wash in cold water.

Emotional stress

Amazonite. Hold onto Amazonite when you feel under stress and emotionally frail. Cup your hand over the stone and bring it toward the solar plexus. You may feel sick at this point as Amazonite is stimulating the chakra. Now push the stone out and visualise a circle of the stone extending around you. Within this circle you will feel emotionally protected while the stone works on the cause of the stress. To become emotionally in control is an ideal but, if you are sensitive, it is a great help to know that there is something you can do positively to aid your vulnerability. Try this exercise whenever you feel under stress.

Moss Agate. Bridges the mental and emotional bodies, allowing gentle integration. It gives one courage to face the truth. Use to hold and breathe into. Brings one's emotions under control whilst grounding stress.

Red Jasper. This stone is good for grounding and for those who are easily flustered. It aids the body in balancing the emotions allowing one to gain control over one's responses. Worn as a pendant, and kept in the pocket. Jasper stones make excellent worry beads. Brecciated Jasper is Jasper with Hematite running through it, and is stronger for those who need more help with emotional stress. Hematite is considered masculine while Jasper is considered feminine. This would help explain why together they complement each other.

Emphysema

Labradorite. I have found that those who suffer from emphysema benefit tremendously from wearing Labradorite. Keep a piece in the room you use for meditation. A Labradorite sphere, once programmed, makes a wonderful healing tool. The stone needs to be near your lungs so I would suggest that you wear it in your bra if you are a woman or keep it in a little pouch around your neck if a man.

Epilepsy

Malachite. Wear on the chest, as jewellery, and keep a piece of tumbled Malachite to hold during meditation. The energy of Malachite is an all round healer. Rub Malachite on the temples when under stress to take the tension away.

Exhaustion

Aragonite. When feeling totally exhausted and in need of peace and quiet, Aragonite gives one the permission to put themselves first. It identifies with the natural early warning system of the body. Work with Aragonite. Hold and meditate with it and allow yourself the luxury of finding your true self.

Eyes

Aventurine. A soothing healer to ease tired and strained eyes. Hold tumbled Aventurine on the temples. Use to meditate with and wear as jewellery.

Blue Agate. Hold in your leading hand. Inhale pure energy, exhale stale energy. Keep your breathing regular whilst concentrating on the Blue Agate. It seems to act like a sieve and filters eye tensions and stress. Blue Agate has a dense, strong energy which relates to the brow chakra. This makes it a wonderful healer for all eye complaints.

Green Agate. So soothing and fresh, Green Agate makes a good energy balancer and works hard on the heart, throat and brow chakras. It generates a different frequency from the Blue Agate and by placing it behind the head, just under the skull, it seems to take eye pain and stress away from the area behind the eyes. Then it channels that pain down the spine and disperses it around the body until it becomes grounded.

Optical Calcite. To meditate with.

Aquamarine. Carry a piece of this crystal in your pocket for clarity of mind. Helps one to reduce mental activity – a common problem of stress. Aquamarine is a wonderful emotional balancer, helping one to cope with phobias and guilt complexes. Very soothing, bringing with it peace and acceptance.

Fatigue

Citrine. Citrine gathers negative energy and never needs cleansing. It prevents self-destructive patterns forming and vibrates at a high pitch working the subconscious faculties. Before long you feel stronger and more determined as ideas start to flow. Brings a sense of light-heartedness. Good at working on the self-esteem and promotes energy. Wear it as a pendant or a ring and keep some in your pocket or purse. It can be placed in your drinking water and used as an energiser. Not so good on the bedside table as you may find you cannot sleep.

Clear Quartz Crystal. This is always a good standby for any ailment as it can be easily cleansed and programmed.

Fear

Moonstone. This is the stone of the Moon goddess. Any female requiring aid in times of great fear has the god-given right to call for the aid of the Moon goddess herself. She will always respond. Any male wishing to call upon the goddess must approach through his female side and prove his worth through respect. The Moonstone is a wonderful comforter and by holding or tumbling it through your fingers it dissipates fear by rationalising the cause.

Prehnite. Because it comes from the darkness and yet is so luminous, its energy knocks and jars at the energy of fear. I have found that it is a great friend when it comes to tackling the things that frighten us most. Keep it in the home or work place and hold it every day telling it why you are scared. It has an uncanny way of making your fears go away.

Fertility

Chrysophase. A true woman's friend and companion. Wear as jewellery and keep a piece for meditation. Excellent for work on the reproductive organs and the heart. They say that if you acquire an egg shaped piece of Chrysophase you will hear of a birth in the family. That is not to say it will be you, but I'm sure you would enjoy working on it.

Flushes, hot and cold

Epidote. Good to tumble in the pocket when you feel yourself begin to flush. If it is more than just an annoyance, place some around you when you relax. Use maybe six or eight pieces to form a circle, then visualise a flow of energy around them. Whilst sat in the centre of this energy circle, visualise a flush of pure energy coming down from above like a huge wave. Let it surge through the chakras and when it hits your feet allow it to bounce back up and out of your head into the universe. This will bring a thorough cleansing with it. Do it three or four times every night for two weeks and monitor the number of flushes you had before the exercise and then after. Next do the same exercise but this time, if it is hot flushes you suffer from, imagine the wave being of ice cold water. If you suffer with cold flushes imagine hot water. Continue for two more weeks still monitoring your progress. After the month is over with, the hard work is done. From then on, whenever you feel a hot flush coming you will automatically visualise a cold wave surge through you and it will counteract the hot flush. Vice versa with a cold flush. Carry a piece of Epidote with you until you no longer require it.

Frozen shoulder

Tourmalinated Quartz wand. The energy charge of Tourmalinated Quartz is incredible and works through the tightest of auras to enable what may only start out as a tiny opening, gradually becoming a channel through which a reconnection with source will allow energy to flow. It aids the elimination of destructive patterns that have built up through many lifetimes. When working with a wand for the use of healing a specific area, like a frozen shoulder for example, I find the healing energies are amplified as they are channelled through the wand and into the body. Work about six inches or 15cms away from the body holding your other hand on the other side of the shoulder. Now stroke the wand through the aura around the shoulder in movements toward the heart. Use straight line strokes up the arm over the shoulder and down towards the heart. After several times of this repeated movement stop and wash the crystal. You may have felt a tingling or sensation of heat in the shoulder. Next start at the centre of the spine in mid-back area and stroke the crystal wand outward and upwards towards the shoulder and over and down the arm.

When you reach the hand and fingers take the wand away from the body and shake slightly. Repeat this movement several times more. The wand should not touch the body and must be cleansed after use. Two or three sessions are usually enough to notice a remarkable difference.

Genital infections

Green Calcite. Works on bacterial growth infections among other things. Place a piece of Green Calcite, about the size of your fist, in front of you. Concentrate on the energy of this mineral. Open yourself up and draw in the vibration, allowing it to enter your body without resistance. Bring the energy down into the base chakra and visualise a grounding of the static sexual energy living there. Green Calcite works on the cause of the condition. While your body is under attack in this centre, it collaborates with the heart chakra to correct the imbalance caused between the two.

Pyrite. Used in the treatment of aggressive and highly infectious diseases, it stimulates the energy of cause and effect kicking in a huge positive blast of energy. Keep around you at work and play. Changes negatives to positives. Can be programmed with the use of a pendulum as a protector!

Goitre

Chrysophase. Wear around the throat chakra. Keep in your pocket and under your pillow when you sleep.

Amber. Wonderfully soothing, the energy from this ancient fossilised resin attunes naturally to the thyroid gland, reducing swelling and easing the condition.

Turquinite. Sometimes known as 'Chinese Turquoise' it is really blue dyed magnesium. However, it has some success with the goitre, perhaps because it relates to a deficiency of iodine in the diet. The recognition of this energy centre's needs stimulates the body's natural healing abilities into action. Carry a few pieces with you and tumble in your hands when you relax. In meditation or as you are drifting off to sleep concentrate on the Turquinite drawing its energy into your thyroid gland.

Grief

Bornite. Better known as Peacock Ore, this iridescent, colourful stone instantly recognises the energy of grief. If you are drawn to it you will be coming to terms with a loss for it has the capacity to lock into an otherwise hidden emotion and bring it out to be dealt with. There is an eventual acceptance that one arrives at when dealing with grief, but it is one that cannot be hurried and each must come at their own pace. Bornite comes out of the Earth dark grey in colour and oxidises to become 'more'. Brightly, iridescently, tarnished in a variety of powerful colours. If returned to the Earth it eventually changes back to dark grey. If you are lucky enough to find a friend within Bornite, cherish it, adore it, love it for it returns your emotions threefold. A great healer for grief.

Hair

Galena. The metallic lustre of Galena makes this a mineral you either like or dislike. It relates to the aura and works on the total energy field of the body. The Latin word for 'lead ore', Galena reduces inflammations and heals the skin. Hold when meditating and concentrate on the area requiring healing. If it is alopecia you are wishing to heal, I found that the Galena brought up many issues of stress to be dealt with before the energy worked on the effect. However, once worked through, a normal growth of hair returned. Baldness is caused by atrophy or exhaustion of the papilla. I have worked with Galena, balancing the aura which has an overall effect on many issues including stabilising hair loss. Wash your hands after using Galena and keep it away from small children.

Unakite Use to ground static energy. Rubbing through the hair improves condition and massages the scalp.

Hormones

Kunzite. Use as an elixir, and to energise your drinking water. Carry some around with you and hold when you go to sleep. Kunzite is a loving crystal that promotes a feeling of peaceful security. It illuminates every particle of your being. Some women during pregnancy find they are drawn to sucking a piece of Kunzite. I have known that true of Moonstone also. Both are good for balancing the hormones.

Chrysophase. A wonderful balancer for the hormones. Use to meditate with and wear as jewellery.

Labradorite. Wear as a pendant or keep a piece of polished Labradorite with you. In a healing, gently take it over the body towards the heart. Labradorite helps to regulate the metabolism, the hormones and overall emotional control. Hold the stone and centre yourself whenever you feel under stress.

Hyperactivity

Dumortierite. Calms the nervous system and cools the release of excitable energy. Dumortierite carried with you eliminates stubbornness and facilitates the ability to see another point of view. Has a grounding effect on static, irrational energy. Dumortierite grounds the overexcited and redirects the energy into a positive mental attitude. Restores composure and roots one into the physical whilst allowing the spiritual to come through without becoming detached.

Moonstone. This milky white to moody black stone is an asset to any healer. But, when working with hyperactivity, I have seen it turn neurotic, irrationally behaved whirlwinds into passive composed angels. Just hold and count slowly to ten.

Immune system

Amethyst. Believed by many to kickstart a slow immune system, Amethyst works on the whole body balancing and regenerating. Use to energise drinking water and wear a large pendant around your neck. It has the very female energy of nurturing and clearing. Stabilises the aura and transmutes negative energy. Meditating with Amethyst or consciously holding the crystal you can program it to assist in the healing of a dysfunctional immune system.

Lapis Lazuli. This ancient stone of mysterious healing powers, when used to meditate with, can aid one in contacting the wisdom of the elders. The tiny flecks of Pyrite within some pieces is said to represent the stars and planets in our solar system. This stone has a powerfully strong energy and when used with intent and purpose can work miracles. Concentrate on the deep blue of the Lapis, feel yourself become one with the energy. Then bring that energy into your body allowing it to work its way into your immune system and pulse through your veins. The energy of Lapis, working in concert with your own, can effect a dramatic change on your well-being for the better.

Infertility

Carnelian. An ancient remedy of the native American. Carry a piece of Carnelian around with you in your pocket or even your medicine pouch. Another remedy of theirs is for the men to run for several miles chewing a piece of pinon pine resin. Whatever it takes, don't question it I suppose!

Fuchsite. The adorable green mineral has success with infertility just by having it around the home. It brings with it information about just what is required for a successful union. A good balancer of red and white blood cells, the hormones and emotions. Try to meditate with this mineral – it has a calming influence.

Insomnia

Howlite. Hold in your hands when you're seeking a peaceful night's sleep. Close your eyes and feel the stones in your palms. At first you will think it is your heartbeat you can feel pulsating in your hands. Now let go of the stones, keeping your eyes closed. Try and feel the pulse in your hands without the stones. After a minute or two hold your stones again and this time note the pace of the beat. You become aware that the stones seem to have a pulse of their own, more striking, perhaps, is that it attunes to you and, after a while, when your energy level has reduced enough to allow sleep, you will notice the pulse in the stones begin to slow. The more you tune in to the stones the slower it becomes – and before you know it you're asleep.

Intestinal 'flu

Pyrite. Good to hold and meditate with. Moves things quickly through the system.

Kundalini energy

Moldavite. The 'stone of transformation'. Used to shift energy, clear blockages and move awareness forward. Good to hold and meditate with. It stimulates the kundalini energy and connects us to the universe.

Stichtite. Works on the kundalini and movement through the chakras. In other words shifts one's concepts and reality. It has the capacity to shift the thoughts from self and slow, low energy to a much faster vibration leaving little time to contemplate. Meditate with this mineral and sleep with it under your pillow.

Sugilite. Place on the third eye and meditate, drawing down spiritual energy whilst stimulating kundalini energy. A great connection to source, this mineral brings a realisation of connection to all things. Makes a good mentor. Often found in elaborate jewellery paying respect to this powerful stone. Often seen exquisitely cut into native American artefacts.

Tektite. An interesting mineral from the outer limits of time and space. It could also be a piece of volcanic rock hurled out of our atmosphere and reentering again, changing its formation. A 'transformation' as our native American elders say. Either way this mineral effects the human energy field in the same way. It transforms the kundalini energy, enabling it to rise through the natural order of the chakras. Tektites also have a more direct effect on telesomatic energy. They accentuate the healer's natural abilities – helping to establish clearer communication.

Larynx

Kyanite. Blue Kyanite is used for healing and strengthening the throat and larynx. A friend to singers and performers, it aligns all chakras naturally. Particularly successful with crown, third eye and throat chakras. The blades of Kyanite, when taken through the aura, allow one to cut through illusion by working within the dimensions that structure one's thinking. After a healing using this technique one feels emotionally lighter and suddenly more creative as if the 'ki' energy connection is restored. Some people will wear a Kyanite pendant to aid the throat chakra and stimulate creative communication.

Lethargy

Geodes. Used to meditate with, they bounce back spiritual energy and stimulate positive thought patterns.

Peridot. Peridot is believed to be an excellent anti-toxin gemstone. It cleans most organs and glands and is a good overall tonic for the body and mind. It reduces stress, accelerates personal growth, stimulates the mind and opens new doors of awareness and opportunity while banishing lethargy and laziness. Use as a focus whilst meditating, or wear in a piece of jewellery.

Leukaemia

Bloodstone. Has been used in the treatment of leukaemia, purifying the blood and clearing toxins. It aids the function of the liver, intestines and bladder, and relates to the sacral and heart chakras. The mineral Bloodstone is a member of the Jasper family and is associated with many gifts. It has mystical properties attributed to it like being able to give one control over spirit energies, dispelling evil and banishing negativity. Find some drilled pieces of Bloodstone and wear them around the neck. Keep some pieces in your crystal pouch. Use to hold and concentrate on when meditating – visualising a reversal of the disease. Place in a dish of water close by your bed at nighttime. Whilst you sleep, it is believed, the leukaemia will be drawn out of your body. In the morning go out into nature and take the water and Bloodstone. Offer it back to the Earth Mother asking her to take it away and break it down. Then bury the stone in the ground. I have never been able to find any of the stones again, so take them away she must.

Loneliness

Herkimer Diamond. When one is missing the person they love then a simple remedy is to buy two Herkimer Diamonds. When two Herkimers are held together by two people – and then one kept by each of them – the stones will retain their attunement no matter how far they are separated – thus maintaining a link between the two holders. When one needs to feel the other just hold the Herkimer.

Love

Celestine. The angelic realms connect to this vibration. Astral travel is facilitated and universal love is attuned to. A definite 'must' for one's crystal collection.

Rose Quartz. Before one can truly love another one must first learn to love themselves. The subtle energies of Rose Quartz heal abuse, guilt, addictions and all the emotions that surround self-worth. A trusting experience that guides one to believe in themselves. Then the vibration lifts and, as one's own energy follows, they become illuminated by the energy and at peace with love. Surround yourself with Rose Quartz. It is an enlightening experience.

Serpentine. Mystery, ceremony, inner beauty and trust. Serpentine is all these things and more. An energy to connect to or aspire to. The magnetism of this energy brings intimacy and love by mirroring and amplifying the vibration. Use Serpentine to meditate with, get used to its energy. It can teach one much about the emotion of love.

Lungs

Aqua Calcite. Works on the breathing, the lungs and life force, Use to meditate with and keep around you in the home. A smooth piece is good to sleep with. The energy of Aqua Calcite stimulates a cleansing and clearing of the chakras.

Sunstone. This might seem a strange choice but Sunstone is believed to be the bringer of life. It energises all chakras and cleanses the entire body. Meditate with a piece of this mineral and bring that life force into the very breath of your existence.

Lymph

Blue Lace Agate. This stone has a gentle cleansing action. It is a stubborn little worker on the nervous system and the lymph glands, clearing blockages and creating movement. Use to hold and meditate with. Place on the navel when relaxing and allow your body to detoxify.

Rose Quartz. Rose Quartz is widely believed to emit a calming, cooling energy that works on all the chakras to gently remove negativity and reinstate the calm. It aids the removal of waste products from the body, clearing and cleansing the lymph glands. A piece of rough Jelly Rose Quartz, that's the beautiful clear Rose Quartz, held during meditation radiates a healing energy that works through the entire body. Then focus on the solar plexus centre and draw the pure, gentle energy into it. As you breathe out, push the energy around that centre and out through the top of your head. Wear Rose Quartz as a pendant or find a pendulum made of this crystal and work on your energy centres with that.

Memory

Emerald. Emerald is said to provide domestic bliss and to instil both sensitivity and loyalty. It can be used to enhance the memory and to stimulate the use of greater mental capacity. Use a piece of rough Emerald to hold and absorb its energy. The gemstone triggers mental acuity and stimulates the memory to work here and now rather then residing in the soul and drawing away. It causes a reaction between your spiritual and physical bodies aiding them to pull together and function together. Have you heard the saying, 'Pull yourself together' or 'Take yourself with you' – well that is exactly what is required when working with the memory.

Moonstone. They say to suck a piece of tumbled Moonstone is good for the memory. However if you forget it is in your mouth you could choke! Better to try it by energising your drinking water, or holding it in your hand. Feeling connected, learning to understand one's shadow or other self and integrating the two. Often a poor memory is teaching us much about our lives, what is important to us and what is superficial. Moonstone helps one understand the importance of 'being'.

Metabolism

Amazonite. This feldspar mineral is generally used to help soothe the nervous system and balance the metabolism. Gives relief to those suffering from emotional and mental stress. Once the nerves and the metabolic rate are under greater control the body can think more clearly allowing one to express oneself creatively. Relieves the feelings of guilt by giving perspective to our most harmful traits and helps us to 'let go'. Buy yourself two or three nice pieces of tumbled Amazonite and use to rub on the body, place in the bath with you and generally get to know. Keep around you and you will find your attention drawn to them throughout the day. Each time, tumble them in your hands.

Apatite. The use of Apatite can help to eliminate overactivity or underactivity by balancing the chakras and clearing blockages. It has proved useful in dealing with hyperactive children and autistic children alike. Apatite also works on the suppression of hunger and the raising of the metabolic rate. Place a piece of Apatite in front of you and concentrate on this stone. Feel its energy and allow it to enter your energy field, directing it around your whole system. Stroke the stone around your aura and hold it to your heart chakra.

Migraine

Aventurine. Weighs and balances the alignment of the intellectual and the emotional bodies, having the ability to shut down either, thus relieving the tension of migraine headaches and soothing the eyes. Red or Green Aventurine works on overactive head energy, and will calmly disperse it given time. It works on the cause of the migraine, not so much the effect, so do not expect immediate reactions. Best to use it as a preventative and carry it with you all the time if you suffer with this nasty complaint.

Smoky Quartz. This is a lovely crystal – cool, calm and dark. It will absorb excessive head activity and ground it. Keep the crystal as cold as possible by having a bowl of ice-cold water next to you. Flush the water away after use. Lie down and close your eyes. Check your breathing pattern and relax. Place a piece of Smoky Quartz on your forehead. Allow your consciousness to be consumed by this cool crystal. As you travel deep into the crystal try not to think or hold onto any thoughts. Slowly a new sense of awareness will become apparent. A highly secretive, almost occult in nature and definitely mystical sense. Allow the feeling of just letting go to take you along without resistance. It can definitely help migraine headaches.

Nerves

Fishtail Selenite. Selenite calms the overexcited, clears the mind gently of troubles and instils peace. It reduces tensions, stabilises emotions and calms the nerves. Place a piece of Fishtail Selenite in your home. Touch it daily and hold it, use it to hold whilst watching the television or listening to music. You will find yourself drifting off and your nerves will become calmer and calmer.

Picture Jasper. Hold some pieces of tumbled Picture Jasper in your hands and turn them over and over. They are great for taking stress away and calming the nerves.

Obsidian. One of the most effective in absorbing negativity. Needs to be washed often, and works hard. Meditate with Obsidian and it will take you to places never encountered before. Magical and deep, it contains all the records of evolution. Takes stress and nervous tensions away and clears the mind. A great companion for anyone who suffers with their nerves.

Nightmares

Prehnite. Prehnite is excellent in dealing with nightmares, fears and phobias. Because it comes from the darkness and yet is so luminous. Its energy knocks and jars at the energy of fear. It makes one feel secure and safe, allaying troubles that play on our minds. Pieces of tumbled Prehnite are good to keep under our pillow.

Numbness

Fluorite. Superior Fluorite is great at relieving numbness from limbs. It helps sufferers of pins and needles also. Gently rub the stone over the skin.

Obesity

Mica. Mica is found in layers which can be shaved into thin sheets. Mica provides for clarity of thought. The thinner the Mica the more transparent. The same as humans really. Take off all the layers of illusion and what have you got? The original energy. If we don't like that energy then we cover it with illusion. Mica teaches us to find and enjoy our real self, then we can take off the layers we hide behind. Working with Mica, the energy shifts one's own energy and alleviates confusion about who we are. It strengthens one's resolve and halts the tendency to hesitate or run away. Things become less chaotic and frustrations subside. It deals with the root cause of obesity then aids the symptoms.

Osteoporosis

Calcite. Calcite is largely made up of calcium carbonate and it has different vibrations for each colour formation. The density of Black Calcite is good to work with, as is the Yellow or Orange when looking to effect a change in the skeletal structure of the body. I like to just hold Calcite because it has a friendly vibration that is consistently pulsing regularly and steadily, on and on. There is a sort of stability in Calcite with which many are able to attune naturally. Learn to accept Calcite as a friend and it can help balance your meridians and effect healing.

Past life

Anyolite. Anyolite is also known as Ruby in Zoisite, and it can create altered states of consciousness, utilising and amplifying the abilities of the mind. It promotes dreaming and stimulates the connection with, and transmission of, information from one's spiritual guides. In addition it provides for the amplification of one's entire energy field. Used in regression work and past-life recall Ruby in Zoisite allows one to slip behind the veil and retrieve information from soul memory. Hold when meditating and during circle work to connect to this elusive energy flow that is usually just beyond reach.

Apophyllite. Used to facilitate astral travel and to provide a clear and definite connection to the physical body during the travelling. It allows one to send information which is gleaned back to the conscious self, this is one of those stones which helps one to remain totally conscious while experiencing the activities of astral travel. It is often used in past-life recall when one is working through lessons that are reoccurring. The mineral also allows one to see into the future. This is facilitated when one looks sideways into the crystal. It is similar to 'scrying'.

Jet. Jet is used for protection and is as ancient as some of the old beliefs. It is sometimes known as the 'witches' stone'. Worn around the neck, usually with Amber, it protects from the entities of darkness, against illness and violence. There is a lot of superstition about this mineral and it is said that those attracted to it are old souls. Jet has long been used by native Americans to symbolise 'the unknowable'. During circle work it is believed that the wearing of Jet guards the physical body allowing safe spiritual travelling without fear of being possessed. The energy of Jet brings peace and serenity. Many find comfort from simply holding Jet when distressed.

Protection

Sugilite. Keep a piece of Sugilite on your person if you feel you need protection. For those who work in the esoteric fields bravery has nothing to do with it. It is common sense to take responsibility and protect yourself. Often found in pendants to wear around the neck.

Turquoise. Used throughout many cultures as a protector from negativity and evil. Wear as jewellery, keep some in your purse or pocket and place on your altar or meditation table.

Psychic attack

Lapis Lazuli. Used in ancient times as a protector from the evil eye. It is often worn to ward of negativity and protect from psychic attack.

Jade. Black Jade is rather a mystery itself but the energy dispels negative attacks so why question it?

Turquoise. It is widely accepted that Turquoise has exceptional powers of psychic protection and, therefore, should never be handled by anyone but the owner – no matter how close they may be! Many native American tribes associate Turquoise with the energy of Father Sky and will wear elaborate pieces of jewellery inlaid with it to protect them during the night-time when the sky is dark, or at times when, during sacred ceremonies, their spirit roams free as their body rests and waits for them inside the kiva or sweat lodge. Place Turquoise around the bed when sleeping to stop anyone attacking your spiritual body whilst your guard is down.

Rheumatism

Amber. The energy of Amber was well known by our ancestors. It used to be distilled to make a pungent thick oil which was then mixed with a carrier oil to lessen the strength. It was then used to rub into areas of rheumatic pain and sciatica. The energy of Amber can be transferred, however, by crystal healing and working with Amber is very rewarding. Use to meditate with and smooth a piece of Amber over the area of the rheumatism.

Copper. To be worn against the skin or held against painful areas. As it warms it collects the negative vibrations from the body. One should then shake the Copper under cold water. Continue until you feel some relief. Taken through the aura, Copper attracts dispersed pieces of negative energy and gathers them up. Good for grounding.

Self-control

Bismuth. Calms and balances all energy centres, promotes a feeling of stability from within – some call it empowerment. Use it when life knocks you sideways.

Shock

Black Calcite. Wonderful for absorbing trauma and shock. Use it to hang on to when you feel you can't cope. The energy is good to stimulate a stabilising influence and eventually reverse the damaging inward spiral of the negative vibrations.

Moonstone Moonstone is a gentle soother and, for those needing time to come to terms with shock or trauma, it is a friend in your solitude. It gradually balances erratic energies bringing an acceptance.

Sinus

Rhodochrosite. The energies of this mineral align themselves to the energies of the delicate tissues and membranes within the cavities of the face. Rhodochrosite will pulsate at the individual vibration required to sustain an equilibrium. Once achieved, the catalytic effect of the energy will reverse the negative and aid healing. Hold against the sinuses and stroke up toward the eye cavities and over the forehead. Wash in cold water and repeat several times. Do this throughout the day and evening, until relief is felt.

Sorrow/Sadness

Azurite. A dream stone of colour and mystique. This mineral is a trickster amongst the mineral kingdom. It lures you with it's beauty and dignity – you would never expect it to be cunning and play dirty. Once you are intrigued enough to have been taken in, and your guard is down, thinking that it relates to your sadness and is on your side, it starts to work with your own energy – turning it against you like a mirror. For example, you take this beautiful mineral home and decide to quieten yourself and meditate with it. After a while you begin to feel agitated, then stressed and angry. Not understanding why, you decide enough is enough and no stupid bit of rock is going to help you, so you had better pull yourself together and do something about it yourself (movement). Of course you would never admit that your reaction was due to the mineral would you? However, that is exactly what I mean about it being a trickster. Who said crystals have to be all sweetness and light? What they do best is what they are good at, healing. No one said you were going to like their methods. Azurite heals sorrow and sadness, it makes you responsible for that emotion. It has a cost.

Spinal column

Calcite. See Osteoporosis.
Fuchite. Works on the flexibility and strength of the muscles, assisting the support of the spinal column. Aids the alignment

and disperses the tension that restricts movement in the shoulders. Meditate with Fuchite and hold the mineral, it has a peaceful presence about it.

Stress

Amazonite. See Emotional Stress.

Red Jasper. See Emotional Stress.

Hematite. Anger and frustration build up and require an outlet. Holding and turning Hematite over and over in your hands relieves cumulative stress. Worn as a pendant or kept in the pocket, it has the effect of dispersing this type of stress when it arrives.

Prehnite. Prehnite can stop one from taking stress inward. A different way of dealing with stress, but just as dangerous. Prehnite accepts that we are not perfect and we sometimes allow life to get us down. It attunes to the quiet types who hold onto stress and take it within which can cause all sorts of weaknesses on the physical body. Meditate with this lovely mineral daily.

Temper

White Howlite. See Anger.

Peridot. See Anger.

Obsidian. Hold for centring and stabilising the emotions in cases of fiery temper. Collects negative energies and grounds stress. Wash frequently as it can become saturated.

Ruby. Ruby acts as a protector when worn around the neck. I have found that the Star Ruby works especially well for this and alleviates the early stages of temper building up. A preventative gem for those who are highly strung. Ruby brings light into dark areas of one's life and teaches one to see the truth in all things. Something we often choose to ignore, due to fear or pain, and so we live a lie – believing things are better that way. The energy of Ruby gives us the courage to say no.

Toxins

Bloodstone. See also Leukaemia. Bloodstone used in meditations can be programmed to work on clearing toxins from the body. Be prepared, however, to undergo a thorough cleansing and deal with the cause along the way.

Ema Crystals. Known commonly as Dragons Eggs these are, in fact, stream-rolled Quartz and have a clean, clear vibration which responds to the low, weak energy that the body transmits when saturated by toxins. Working with Ema Crystals promotes all round good health and clears negative energies out of the aura.

Trauma

Black Calcite. See Shock.

Moonstone. See Shock.

Garnet. A strong stimulant for those in trauma, it strengthens positive resolve, balances the emotions and warns of danger when you are spiritually weak. Those who carry Garnet with them acquire a rhythm that discourages negativity and chaos. It aids control over the kundalini energy which fluctuates during development causing imbalances. Make a friend of Garnet; it is a strong ally.

Rhodonite. An individual stone that demands respect. I know of a case where, when placed on a television set along with a group of other crystals and minerals, the lady of the house said the Rhodonite would fly across the room. It did not wish to be with the other stones and certainly not on the television. It resided, after that, on a shelf by itself. I am often surprised at the parallels between human and crystal behaviour. Rhodonite is a mineral 'with an attitude'. It is good for balancing yin and yang energy bringing calmness and tranquillity. If you have respect for it, and are prepared to do the work, it will pull you through your worst nightmare. Hold Rhodonite when in a state of deep traumatic shock and let it be your guide.

Tumours

Double Terminated Quartz Crystal. A natural double terminated Clear Quartz point is a wonderful healing tool with many
uses. Tumours are obviously things that cause a lot of worry and
for many reasons one always hopes that they will just go away.
Now, I don't wish to take on the medical profession – and I
know all the arguments about 'offering false hope' in such
serious cases, but I feel strongly that a large part of the healing
comes from the patient themselves – and if someone in such
suffering is brave enough to ask for my help they will get it. I
have used an old wives' tale for working with tumours for
simple reasons. If it works, why question it? Often, by seeking
the answer one may just lose the magic. Take the Crystal point
and move it over the body, feeling the energy field. Work up
from the heart and then down from the heart. Spread the aura
out and open it up where you can. Pull the aura open gently
with one direct movement from the toes up to the crown. Now
you are ready to approach the tumour itself. Begin with a small,
gentle anticlockwise movement with your Double Terminator
Crystal in your leading hand and your empty hand pointed
towards the ground. As you steadily widen the circles you are
trying to loosen the tumour and bring its energy under your
control. The empty hand is there to discharge any negative
energy away from you and into the ground. Then, working over
the tumour, change hands and start to spiral from the centre in
a clockwise direction, taking your time. You should now have
your leading hand under the tumour itself while you continue
to circle with the Double Terminator Crystal in your other hand.
Focus on the tumour, telling it that you are going to take it away
and it must move its energy into the Terminator. As the spirals
get wider, bring it further and further away from the body.
When you feel you have all the energy of the tumour inside the
Terminator, place it in a piece of cotton material and wrap it up.

Wash your hands thoroughly and then, finally, close the aura. Close the 'auric body' first by one swift movement from crown to toe using your Catalyst Crystal. Then place a protective 'shield' around the subject, moving in deliberate clockwise movements, until the energy becomes thick again. If you are working on yourself you may need to rest a while now. Once you have finished the healing take the Double Terminator into nature, a wooded area is fine or a garden. With your hands, no sharp objects, bury the Crystal in the ground, you must have no desire to keep the Crystal and give it freely back to the Earth. An offering is usual and most give bread and wine, a little of each or some give tobacco. A simple sacred prayer asking the Earth to take the tumour away is in order. Then cover the Crystal and leave it to do its work. Done with intent and a pure heart I have seen the 'Crystal and Earth' ceremony work very well. The Crystal programmed to take away the tumour makes sense and so does disposing of it. After all, you wouldn't want to leave it lying around for a loved one to pick up would you?

Warts

Sea Salt. From Full Moon to New Moon rub the wart with Sea Salt. Wash the used Sea Salt down the drain. Do this once each evening for the fourteen days. If it has not gone by the Full Moon, repeat the process.

Wrinkles

Gypsum. Used in beauty therapy rooms etc. Gypsum has a special energy which promotes the elasticity of the skin tissues. A vibration that is slow and positive which makes it a good one to align yourself to if you are wishing for longevity. Known as a rejuvenator, it increases the sex drive and will power.

7

Crystal
tools

Wands

Wands have been used for centuries – if not millennia – by the healers, shaman and mystics of countless civilisations. Even today, children are taught to believe that *'If you're going to do magic – you've got to have a wand!'* Exactly where the idea of wands originated, no one knows. There are references in Sumarian texts to priests and kings carrying their 'wands of power' and the pharaohs of Ancient Egypt were surrounded by high priests – all carrying their 'staff' or wand of office. When Moses was 'sent' by God to face the Pharaoh and compel him to release the Hebrews, God made a point of telling him to carry his staff with him. There can be little doubt that, to our ancestors, the wand was believed to hold terrific powers. The practice, still continued today, of a monarch carrying an orb and sceptre is a continuation of this belief. The spherical orb represents the World, and the wand-like sceptre represents the monarch's spiritual power over it.

The 'subtle physics' behind the wand's power are really deceptively simple. As we have already discussed, our aim – when we administer healing – is to ask that the source energy is passed through us and into the aura of the recipient. Now there is a simple, basic principle of physics that we should all be familiar with. The Italian physicist, Bernoulli, first described the phenomenon in his treatise on 'The Behaviour of Matter'. He stated 'Whenever a flow of matter is compressed or confined, its velocity must accelerate in direct proportion to the amount of restriction and propelling force applied to it.' Put simply, if you restrict the flow of matter (e.g. water through a hose) the speed of the matter will increase (if you pinch the end of the hose the water will flow faster, and with increased power).

So, to visualise this in 'wand' healing, you allow the source energy to start flowing through your aura – passing out through your dominant, or 'giving', hand and into the recipient. Then you place a wand in the palm of your giving hand, closing your fingers around it. Now visualise the source energy rushing through your aura and being compressed, at the point of leaving, into the wand. All that powerful energy is now being compressed, through the wand, into a highly focused beam of energy. The healer now simply directs this beam into the part of the recipient's aura that most needs the additional help.

This technique is particularly helpful when you are working to dispel or 'shift' stubborn blockages in the aura. The recipient will feel a distinct 'tingle' as the concentrated energy enters their aura.

I have met crystal healers who seem to believe that one has to be either a 'wand' healer or a 'stone' healer. I'm afraid that, to me, this attitude is extremely naïve. That is rather like saying that there are 'scalpel' surgeons and there are 'forceps' surgeons – and 'never the twain shall meet'. That, is of course, ridiculous. When I am healing, I care only about the recipient. I allow their needs to dictate entirely which techniques are most appropriate. There are cases when I will rely solely on counselling – just as there are cases when I will use only a wand. We must remember that our own prejudices have to be discarded when we begin to heal another.

Wands themselves come in a wide variety of crystals and formations. There are thousands of variations and, in my experience, you need to experiment until you find the combination that you can work with most comfortably. There will be some crystal wands that, no matter how beneficial they may be for your patient, are simply no good for you. Remember that you have to work extremely closely with the wand and if it's having a harmful effect on you – don't use it. You will not help your patient one bit by making yourself weaker. After some time you may find that you work best with a 'combination' wand constructed from a number of different crystals and bound together using Copper or some equally effective 'conductor'. These can be particularly effective and they are also far more personal. If you are attracted to this type of wand, choose it very carefully. Take great care in identifying every crystal and material used in the making of the wand. I have seen some wands that are exquisite to look at but contain combinations of crystals that actually work against each other – setting up a disharmony within the wand itself. These wands, although beautiful to look at, will be of little help for healing and, in fact, could even worsen the very problems that you are trying to relieve. Perhaps the best maker of such combination wands that I have ever found is a crystal healer himself. His name is John Karal and he takes great care in choosing and constructing each wand. The combinations are extremely powerful to work with and, because of his great artistic talent, strikingly beautiful.

In this chapter, however, I have mainly concentrated on 'natural' wands and their properties. I am always happy to hear from anyone who wants advice on the more exotic combinations.

The Amethyst wand

The Amethyst wand is particularly well suited to working on the energies of the brow centre, coming through the pituitary gland and balancing the chemicals it produces. It also has great success inducing its violet rays into the sacral centre which bring the qualities of 'right relationship'. Start at one of these chakra centres, about two inches away from the body. With your leading hand holding the wand, slowly draw circles over the centre in an anticlockwise direction steadily moving away from the body upwards. Whilst doing this, point your other hand towards the ground and visualise negative energy leaving your body this way. This procedure stops you absorbing the negative energy and allows you to direct it back to the Earth Mother. When this is completed, cup your open hand to bring down the energy of source whilst now drawing clockwise circles above the same energy centre. Whilst doing this, visualise the channel of positive energy flowing into the centre and creating balance.

The Fluorite wand

A beautiful wand, created in Fluorite and stroked across the skin, is an instant healer. It feels and looks every inch a crystal that will relieve suffering and pain. Children are drawn to Fluorite instinctively and they seem to know intuitively how to use it. For example, to relieve swelling and stress in the wrist, start above the body at the fingers and gently guide the crystal towards the pain visualising the wand absorbing the pain. Take the wand up towards the top of the arm and stroke it away from the body. Then shake the crystal gently. Repeat this, each time getting closer to the body, until you feel confident in touching the skin. It is useful to have a small bowl of cold water close by. As the crystal gets warm, wash it in the cold water. Some believe that all the pain is then transferred to the water and after the healing it should be tipped into the Earth for the Earth Mother to 'digest' all the pain. The Fluorite wand can be used effectively on the brow and head centres. It is useful for intellect and balancing brain cells. You should use it on these centres in the same way as described in the Amethyst wand section.

The Obsidian healing wand

The mysterious volcanic glass whose intrinsic properties include truth by the reflection of one's flaws. It improves the clarity of one's vision to observe a clear pathway that will help to navigate the changes necessary to eliminate them. For this reason, Obsidian has built a reputation for itself as a gemstone to be careful with – as the truth can sometimes hurt. The Obsidian wand is a powerful healing tool used to absorb negative energies within the aura and ground the physical body. It is a strong protective stone, clarifying the inner state of the patient and centring them with Earth energy while the healer works. Thus the benefits can be felt almost immediately. The wand will probably need to be cleansed several times during the healing since it is so highly absorbent and it can become saturated very quickly.

The Quartz healing wand

A Clear Quartz point, whether natural or carved, emits both negative and positive energy. It has the ability to change polarity when subjected to heat or pressure and is therefore useful in the balancing of energy around the body by transforming, amplifying or dissipating it. When slowly worked around the body, within the aura, it naturally returns one to balance. Some areas take more time than others and it is up to the experience of the healer to read the etheric signals and relate to them. You need to carefully select a wand, guided by your intuition, since a hand-cut wand requires programming by the healer and such tools should never be shared. These are personal tools that need to be treated with respect and kept wrapped or stored in a pouch when not being used. They need to be cleansed between healings so not to transfer energies and, with time, the more they are used the more powerful they become. Used for rejuvenation, purification and the focus of positive thought, Quartz can enhance the flow of spiritual interaction. It helps in the recognition of disease and ancient priests are said to have programmed Quartz Crystal to render negative energies impotent – essential when identifying the cause of an illness.

The Rose Quartz wand

Rose Quartz is the gentlest of all the wands I have worked with and its peaceful energy restores calm. It works well at slowing down energy centres that are spinning erratically and achieves a calm state of mind. It is a wonderful tool to use in conjunction with reflexology for gently massaging the points on the foot relating to the stress areas on the body. It can be used on all centres of the body in the same way as described in the Amethyst wand section.

The Smoky Selenite wand

A rare combination of Smoky Quartz surrounded by Fishtail Selenite. The healing properties of a wand like this combine both energies of Smoky Quartz and Selenite making this a truly magical piece. These wands are gentle teachers of energy balancing. They are best used following an emotional break-down, trauma or extreme stress that has necessitated healing. They penetrate a tight, protective aura and work through the entire cell structure – leaving a feeling of total cleansing.

The Smoky Quartz wand

The soothing energy of Smoky Quartz makes a wand that is an excellent addition to any healer's collection. It works well, grounding base chakra energy by connecting it to the feet centres to restore proper direction flow. Stand over your patient and, with your leading hand holding the wand, describe a circle from the feet up to the base chakra and then back down to the feet again in an anticlockwise direction. Don't forget to keep your open hand pointed towards the ground and visualise negative energy leaving through your fingers into the ground. Send them back for the Earth Mother to deal with. When you feel that this has been achieved, cup your open hand to receive healing energy from source and draw in the energy to the centres by now circling clockwise. Do this until you feel a calmness enter the centre. By doing this you will also relieve head tensions by equalising the energy flow away from the head.

The Tourmalinated Quartz wand

This is, without question, one of the most powerful of the healing tools used by healers around the world. Its energy charge is incredible and works through the tightest of auras to enable what may begin as just a tiny opening, gradually widening into a channel through which this reconnection with source will allow energy to flow. It helps eliminate destructive patterns that have built up through many lifetimes. It also assists by showing us the negative and destructive patterns that exist within our own nature and not only helps us face them but also helps us deal with them. This beautiful wand relates to each of the chakras, clearing, maintaining and stimulating them. It encourages self-confidence and self-worth and provides for the protection of the healer as well as the patient. It balances all the meridians of the physical body

Pyramids – toys or tools?

The sacred pyramid shape has fascinated the imagination of scientists and scholars alike. Believed by some to be used for sacred rituals, to summon and entrap energies that would then be used, like a 'highly charged battery', by the high priest or priestess. The crystal pyramid, when used as a focal point in meditation, can be programmed to do exactly that. Charge the pyramid with positive healing energies when working in circle then, when healing is required, hold the pyramid and ask for the energies to be released. The crystal will only recognise your own vibration and so only you can access the power within the crystal pyramid. If you wish to work on the chakras, place the pyramid on the relevant chakra when lying down. Then it is up to your visualisation, will and intent. Powerful geometric forms are able to access extraordinary energies – and those who choose to work with pyramids will find them a truly magical experience.

Many people are so fascinated by crystal pyramids that they feel good just holding them. Most use them for meditation purposes. In recent years more and more crystals and minerals cut into this shape have come on to the market to meet growing demand. Marble and onyx have been favourites with black and gold being very popular. They have come in a variety of sizes, but be warned, if they get over 15 to 20 cms in height they become extremely heavy. Smaller pyramids of just a few centimetres are perfect and today they can be found in most crystal types with Tourmalinalated Quartz being one of the most powerful and intriguing.

A Fluorite crystal pyramid works an the heart, throat and third eye chakras beautifully – stimulating movement and clearing blockages. It feels like it is drawing and absorbing negative energy from the centre and many have imagined that dark strands of a sticky liquorice-like fibre have been dragged out of these centres leaving the chakra untangled and clear. It is great for stimulating movement on the third eye. It can accelerate astral projection and travellings of the spirit. Fluorite encourages the process of correlating information retrieved during such experiences into a structure one can comprehend. The Fluorite pyramid acts as a memory bank and stores this information within its many chambers until you access it by achieving a level of understanding. Personal advancement is propelled by working with this crystal shape as it helps us to grasp the 'universal picture' as a whole and attune to the higher vibrations. It also pushes us to accept change. Sometimes we feel we are ready and eager to move forward and yet our subconscious resists. Fluorite helps us to work through this and although we might feel we are going backwards – we are actually moving forward.

A Smoky Quartz crystal pyramid is so soothing. It radiates peace and calm, grounding head stress and tensions. To meditate with it is a joy. Use it on the forehead to access the dream state and 'dream walk' experience.

These are just a few examples of the amazing powers of the crystal pyramid. I do not propose to dwell on the multitude of crystal formations available in the pyramid shape. You'll find that half of the fun and enlightenment comes from your own voyage of discovery. You should experiment and research the ones that feel right for you.

Special property crystals

Record keeper crystals

Occasionally one will come across the term 'record keeper' crystals whilst studying crystal energy. These are generally natural Clear Quartz Crystal points that have slightly raised or grooved triangles on one or more of the faces which can be clearly seen in the light. Turn the crystal slowly and watch the play of light up and down one face at a time. In a record keeper crystal you will see one or more triangle shapes. The shape of the triangles can vary widely but, it is believed, the most precious are those carrying one or more perfect equilateral triangles. It appears that this is the key to unlocking their store of knowledge. Only when the triangles have formed themselves into a perfect equilateral shape is the crystal ready to divulge its knowledge. These are the much spoken about crystals that carry the imprint of the entire evolution of the planet within their 'libraries'. Access to this sacred knowledge is through contemplation and meditation. It is said that a connection to the Akashic records themselves can be achieved by meditation with a record keeper. When enough of these sacred crystals have been found and activated, by the awareness of mankind, some believe that they will lead us to powerful locations on the Earth which are 'doorways' to higher realms.

Personally I feel more comfortable with the belief that these special crystals, if you are lucky enough to have one come into your possession, will help you unlock the doorways into your inner self on the journey toward self-realisation. They act as a catalyst, removing blockages within the psyche that enable you to gain a deeper understanding of yourself – your successes and failings – strengths and weaknesses – and to come to terms with your own power.

Phantom crystals

These are easily recognised by the 'phantom' literally growing inside the 'mother' crystal. They occur in Quartz Crystal formations, sometimes singular – sometimes in clusters. They are formed by massive shifts in the Earth's crust. For example –

a smoky 'phantom' in Clear Quartz is probably the result of an upheaval that threw the formation several thousand feet higher on the crust. When the crystal was growing closer to the heat of the Earth's core, it was smoky in character. After being shifted away from the heat it continued to grow – but without the heat it became clear. The result is a crystal formation where dark grey crystal can be easily seen within the Clear Quartz cluster. Sometimes the phantom will be caused by another mineral 'overgrowing' a Quartz. I have seen some spectacular Smoky-Selenite phantoms from China. The Smoky Quartz was overgrown entirely by striated Selenite. Some of these samples even had minute channels of water trapped in them. It's fascinating to see a tiny bubble of water that you know became trapped several million years ago. These unique crystals are often used by healers for distance healing. They are placed in front of the healer during meditation. The focus is on the phantom – the phantom represents the person requiring the healing. Throughout the healing, unconditional love is sent directly to the patient via the crystal, which acts like an amplifier directing the collective energies of the crystal and the healer to the patient. After a number of these sittings the crystal is usually sent to the patient where it finishes the healing 'job' by being in close proximity to the recipient.

Partner crystals

These are two individual crystals that have grown together. Their points lie alongside each other facing the same way. They look like a couple lying side by side. It is considered a good partner crystal if one is slightly larger then the other. Some partner crystals have their points reversed and are considered to be in balance with one another. Occasionally the points are at a tangent to each other and these are usually in respect of the relationship of mother/daughter, father/son etc. It is usual to buy a partner crystal for your loved one as a token of your feelings and your wish to always be close. Some people buy them for themselves when they are lonely and desire to find a loving partner. It is a crystal often sought after for love magic.

Window crystals

A window crystal is identified by finding a small diamond-shaped window within a crystal termination. Sometimes it is just beneath the surface and occasionally it may be deep within. It is believed that by meditating and focusing on the window one can travel through the window and transcend time and space. With practice one can gain control of this ability and, at will, journey deep into the mind and subconscious unlocking the mysteries held there. Rather like the record keeper it can be used as a doorway into other realms and as a connection to access into the akashic records. The akashic records are the atoms of energy that hold the memory of every thought and action that has ever happened or is ever likely to happen.

8

Crystal
configurations

I have covered many aspects of healing with crystals within
the pages so far. Some are very simple procedures that require
nothing more than compassion, intuition and a little patience.
Others require knowledge of channelling and healing
techniques that are, in many ways, similar to many alternative
practices. They represent the application of common sense,
more than anything, and become second nature very quickly.
Indeed, once you have started to relate to concepts like
channelling, auras, chakras, etheric bodies, reincarnation and

karma, your awareness will start to expand at a phenomenal rate as you hunger for more input. Once the veil is lifted, it becomes the introduction to so many cross-cultural beliefs and philosophies to which, today, we are fortunate enough to have access. Crystal healing, colour healing, rebirthing, feng-shui, homeopathy, aromatherapy and herbalism. 'Mediumship' alone divides into transmediums, clairvoyant mediums, clairaudiant mediums. The list seems endless and we can only wish to simply inhale all this new exciting information that has been hidden or inaccessible for too long. But don't be too impatient to arrive at the journey's end. The speed at which we travel is irrelevant. It is 'going in the right direction' that really matters and when you finally arrive at your destination, only to realise that it is just a doorway into yet another journey, you may wish that you had spent a little more time 'enjoying the ride'.

I suppose this is my way of preparing you for the next 'ride' because the concepts involved in crystal configurations can be either the hardest or simplest concept to grasp in crystal healing. It really only requires that you have taken on board all that has been said about responsibility. It is of the utmost importance that we start with an awareness that there is a 'natural' order of progression through the chakras. This has been acknowledged by healers, mystics and shaman for thousands of years, passed on by oral tradition up to the present. It is discussed in groups, circles and sects across the globe who wish to share and expand their knowledge. It is often considered to be a valuable key to understanding the spiritual evolution of mankind. This 'natural' progression brings the energy centres into complete alignment, leading to a more natural state of being. This, in turn, frees us from the neurotic aspects of emotions and attachments to 'dualistic' concepts. Even though this is our actual natural state, it can still be exceptionally difficult to achieve as we each have many habitual patterns to deal with. These patterns are what karma is all about rather than the simplistic view of punishment and reward. This has helped me greatly in understanding myself and why I seemed compelled to continually repeat the same mistakes in this life-time. I've probably been going around in circles for many lifetimes in fact, just to deal with one fundamental concept. Many healers believe that the lesson gets harder each time we fail to grasp the concept we are dealing with until, through necessity, we eventually take notice.

One healer I worked with told me that through her work she came to realise that we each have a 'guardian angel' that stays with us through our lifetime on the Earth. This angel's duty is to make sure that we remember what it is that we have come back to do. The angel watches over us and nudges us in the right direction or presents us with opportunities in order that we take notice. However if we continually make the same mistake, through our own wilfulness and inability to learn, the healer believed that God pairs us with another soul trying to learn the same lesson. This is because there are not enough angels to go around and even though one angel can, at any moment in time, have many students to watch over, rather then take up their time continually on the same issue, God decides that we need to experience both sides of this equation. So that we could realise just how difficult it was to get one 'half-asleep' human to trust their intuition, one soul would reincarnate and the other would take on the role of guardian angel. At the end of that lifetime they would swap roles. But, of course, that could mean that our guardian angel may be no more 'clued-up' than we are. In fact they could very well be less aware than ourselves and we would need to learn the lesson of compassion because otherwise it would be just a rather pointless 'merry-go-round'. It is, I have to admit, a fascinating idea and may have some sort of merit – if not in the purely religious context that she meant it. I am more inclined to believe that our guardian angel is a form of our higher self, our total sum of energy that makes up our invisible body that is a living entity all the time unlike the physical body that is only physical some of the time. This would account for our conscience and our connection to the energy of the universe – the 'source'.

Natural progression through the chakras means to work through all the complexities of human nature and, as each chakra symbolises a facet of that nature, the rewards are great. It would mean evolving to our highest state of 'being' – living in harmony with the planet and the cosmos. The realisation that the chakras, though an illusion, are necessary for us to relate to in order to understand the finer balance between ourselves and all that is. If we were to take the body to pieces no chakras would be found since these represent our connection to the etheric body. Energy flows through these centres when they are in balance and this is commonly called the 'kundalini'. This energy only naturally flows when the centres are fully stabilised in a specific order. The correct order of alignment should be:

Sacral – First chakra in alignment
Solar plexus – Second chakra in alignment
Brow – Third chakra in alignment
Base – Fourth chakra in alignment
Crown – Fifth chakra in alignment
Throat – Sixth chakra in alignment
Heart – Seventh chakra in alignment

The kundalini only naturally begins to flow through the body at the stages where the base and then the crown are stabilised i.e. the fourth and fifth stages. At the end there is no concept of kundalini whatsoever. There is only the unified state. Therefore, in reality, no 'serpent' to be awoken in the first place. That is only the illusion of separation.

A wrong order of alignment, for example, would be to pull the kundalini energy up from the base chakra which creates grandiose illusions of power and the possibility of madness. (This happens when we wish to progress too fast and go the 'wrong way'.) It is of extreme importance that the progression of energy through the chakras is handled with knowledge. It can be dangerous to dabble with kundalini energy if one has little experience or understanding of it. As to the concept of the kundalini being pushed, I would recommend that you leave this area well alone. Many inexperienced occultists have created problems beyond their control by believing that the serpent needs to be awakened and then raised.

It is, in fact, the heart chakra where emotion is born. That stimulates the sacral chakra into action and it is here that the first stirrings of awareness are felt. It is also the heart chakra which must be the last centre to align. Many believe that this is the meaning behind the words 'the Alpha and the Omega – the beginning and the end'. It is the natural opening up of the chakras that brings one to awareness.

It is important to only work on the chakras along the spine i.e. the back of the person, as this way a lower centre corresponds to a higher one. It is an upward progressive movement. If we were to work on the chakras at the front of the body, it would pull the higher centres down into the lower ones – a 'regression' instead of a 'progression'.

These are what we believe to be the fundamental esoteric laws of healing that have been observed throughout the ages. If kundalini is forced upwards from the base, this produces a premature burning and destroys the protective webs connecting the chakras in the body. These are the connections through to the etheric body which hold our spiritual energy in place. If these are 'burned out' we have little protection on the astral plane. We are then left open to 'walk-ins' – entities attracted to our energy as it leaks out into the ether. These can be negative or positive, though most are considered to be negative due to their presence on the lower planes.

My knowledge of crystal configurations comes from working with other healers and experimenting with them over many years. I feel that this subject holds the potential for a lifetime's study alone, experimenting with all the various crystals and minerals and different placements of stones around and on the body. There are two main categories of healing with crystal configurations. Firstly, there are geometric patterns – laid out and charged with an energy flow – that you can construct for yourself. Once this is done, you lay inside the formation and relax, allowing the crystals to cleanse and balance you. Secondly, there are the crystal configurations that need to be constructed so that you, the healer, can then work within the formation on specific chakras.

For configuration work, I usually use only Clear Quartz crystals, whether tumbled, single terminated points or occasionally double terminated. If you wish to perform configuration work you will need a selection of these. They're referred to as the 'subsidiary crystals'. You will also need a 'catalyst crystal', very often a wand, which you should keep as your personal crystal. This crystal should be treated with respect and kept for your own personal use.

General guidelines to working with configurations

• Make sure that a protective shield of energy is placed around the body in some form.

- Make sure that you align your will to the highest good so the chakras only receive the amount of energy that is correct for the recipient at that time.
- Make sure that you always energetically go around a configuration clockwise with your catalyst crystal. (This is because it is an 'evolutionary' movement – never go around anticlockwise as this would be 'devolutionary'.)
- Never attempt to raise the kundalini energy.
- Always energise the chakra centres in the correct sequence along the spine – from the back.
- Always make sure your patient is well grounded before leaving.
- After every healing session – cleanse your tools thoroughly.

If the patient is able to lay comfortably on the floor, using a mat, it gives space for crystals to be laid on and around the body in 'gridlines'. At our healing centre, in Glastonbury, we have discovered that there are two, intersecting 'ley lines' running through our healing rooms. These are proving very effective, clearing chakra blockages at a phenomenal rate and they even seem to amplify the properties of crystal tools. The results have been amazing. By laying a patient along the ley line and placing crystals at strategic points, it is possible to balance all the energy centres of the body by flushing them with energy.

There are three elements that seem to be important in using this 'ley' energy. You have to be aware of the direction of the ley line, the direction of the energy flow within the ley line and, depending on the time of year, the appropriate amount of time that the patient should remain within it. With practice, we have learnt that some patients need to lay 'North–South' while others benefit more from being laid 'South–North'. There appears to be a negative or positive charge within the ley line and the needs of each patient differ. No longer than twenty minutes seems a correct 'rule of thumb' although, at times when the energy is particularly strong, such as leading up to Summer Solstice, it would be far too long and a few minutes would be enough. People of a nervous disposition and children would probably find this energy a bit overwhelming and I would not recommend this method for them. Many patients during this form of healing can burst into tears, exhibit flatulence or feel a little 'woozy'. This is the body's way of ridding itself of blockages that manifest in a physical way and shows the success of the healing process.

The 'Vesica Piscis' crystal configuration

This is a superb configuration (see Figure 5), appropriate for almost all healing conditions. The root of disharmony is imbalance and wrong-relationship between some, or even all, of the energy centres. This configuration also is a good example of how one chakra works with another. It involves the awakening of the brow chakra. Essentially, that is the very beginning of illumination, which is healing in itself. Because of the specific order in the progression of these centres we can relate this process to the development of a baby. Life, in the physical world, begins at the sacral chakra and, almost immediately, progresses to the throat chakra. This is because we are conceived in the sacral – which is a physical centre. A newborn baby has no connection, at this point, with any other chakra except the crown. It cannot yet talk so the throat chakra is still undeveloped. It does not yet understand the concept of heart connections to the world, such as compassion etc., so the heart chakra is undeveloped. There is no concept yet of power or aspiration, which relate to the solar plexus. There are no survival instincts yet and so it has no connection to the base chakra. It has no sense of perception and so the brow chakra is still undeveloped. The crown chakra is crucial because without it, we could not 'draw in' the source energy needed to activate our other chakras. It maintains our connection to source and the universe. It seems to become active at the moment of birth, although it can often take more than a lifetime to understand its connection to the other chakras. Only after all other chakras are aligned and connected can we realise the role of the crown chakra as the focal point of our energy centres, working in synchronicity along the spine.

Following the 'birth' rationale, I have come to accept the concept that the throat chakra develops an alignment to the sacral chakra as the inner energy flow seeks to communicate itself. Then the solar plexus aligns to the heart as it aspires towards growth and the development of heart-felt relationships with its environment – beginning with the mother. The base chakra next aligns to the crown, representing the developing survival instinct of the base corresponding to the 'higher will' and intelligence of the crown. The brow is then naturally activated once the base and crown have aligned, as imagination joins with intellect.

Now all we need to know is how to lay the crystals out in order to achieve this balance. I find this configuration best because it most completely reinforces the natural order of alignment that we experienced at birth and then seemed to 'lose' as we grew in the physical world. It is all a question of remembering the placement order of the crystals. I relate to this shape easily since it is also the symbol of Glastonbury's famous 'Chalice Well'.

How to lay the crystals out

The 'Vesica Piscis' configuration is so called because, when drawn on a piece of paper, it primarily consists of two, large overlapping circles with two smaller circles within this. You will need sixteen single-terminated Quartz crystals plus your own catalyst crystal to use this configuration.

Ask your patient to lay face down in a comfortable position and become aware of their breathing for a few minutes. Suggest that they visualise inhaling pure energy, white light or something that they relate to as healing breath. On the exhaled breath, suggest that they visualise exhaling negative energy. While they settle, place a large protective shield around them. You could, for this, simply visualise a circle of light. Spend a moment aligning your will to the highest good and ask that the patient only receives that which they need at the time. This has as much to do with you as it does your patient. You do not want to interfere with universal laws. Now, take your catalyst crystal in your leading hand and, with one swift movement from top to bottom, 'unzip' the auric field. Visualise it like a big sleeping bag or cocoon being opened. Next, place your sixteen crystals, around and on the body, corresponding to the arrows in the diagram (see Figure 5). The points of the terminators should all be pointing upwards and there are four crystals to each circle. The first circle should be sacral to throat. The second should be solar plexus to heart. The third should be base to crown and last from beneath the feet to the sacral. Once they are all in place, take your catalyst crystal in your leading hand again and, at about two inches from the body, start to 'draw in' the circles. Always draw them in two halves from the lower chakra to the higher chakra. With your other hand cupped, visualise receiving healing energy in and directing it out through the catalyst crystal. Draw each circle slowly and patiently about four times. Then stop and, sitting quietly, allow the crystals to do their work for about twenty minutes.

Afterwards, carefully remove the crystals in the opposite order to that in which they were placed and, with your catalyst crystal, make one swift movement from bottom to top. This will close the auric field that you opened at the start. Do not think of this as 'sealing' the aura – it is merely putting things back as they were before. A surgeon would not leave a patient with an open wound. Do not 'zip' around the whole body or over the crown. The aura is a living breathing entity and needs to be connected to all things. Finally, draw large circles around the patient several times until you feel the energy becoming thicker. I always touch the patient gently on the shoulder to let them know the healing session is over and allow them a few minutes to ground themselves and come around. At this point I always offer thanks to the great source and mentally separate our two auras. You should offer water and check that the patient is happy and responsive. If not, suggest that they rub their hands together or stamp their feet. Some people do experience difficulties with their faculties after returning from a state of deep relaxation so be patient. I find that some like to talk a little while others like to be left alone for a short time to reflect. This configuration normally leaves the patient feeling light and relaxed. Repeated weekly for six weeks or so, a marked improvement is usually evident.

I love this configuration because, when I am using it, I visualise that I am in the Chalice Well gardens on a warm, sunny day. I can hear the leaves on the trees rustling in the wind, which is the energy required to create movement, and I can hear the running of the water, which is necessary for a cleansing to take place. Above all I can feel the peace that resides in the beautiful gardens enter the patient and gently it begins to balance and heal them. All the elementals are present in the

Chalice Well gardens, waiting to be tapped into. People travel far and wide to visit and experience their gentle healing qualities.

The Triangulation configuration

This configuration (see Figure 6) is excellent for the alignment of the chakras, and requires three single-terminator Quartz points plus, of course, your catalyst crystal. Once your patient is laying down in a comfortable position, ask them to become aware of their breathing for a few minutes. As always, spend a moment aligning your will to the highest good – asking that the patient only receives that which is essential to their needs. Place two of the single termination Quartz crystal points at the feet, one at each foot pointing up towards the body. Place one at the crown chakra slightly above the head pointing outward away from the crown (see Figure 6). Using your catalyst crystal in your leading hand go around in a clockwise direction to join up the crystal points. Next open the auric field by doing one swift movement with your catalyst crystal from head to toe. Now, swap hands and point your leading hand down towards the ground to direct negative energy away from the body and visualise this going back to the Earth Mother. With your other hand holding the catalyst crystal, work anticlockwise on the energy centres in this order: sacral, solar plexus, brow, base, crown, throat and heart. This is to draw out the negative energies and ground them. Do several careful circular motions on each centre and try not to hurry this – some centres may take longer than others. Now, change hands again. Take your crystal in your leading hand and turn your other hand palm-upwards to draw down energy from source. This time, describe clockwise motions on the chakras to feed them. Once again, take your time. Spend the time necessary on each centre, working in the same order as before.

When this is over, make one swift motion from toe to crown with your catalyst crystal to place everything back just as it was. Then, calmly, draw large clockwise circles around the patient until their energy becomes thick again. Finish the healing as with the Vesica Piscis configuration.

The Pentagram configuration

One configuration that has proven particularly powerful in balancing the aura is the Pentagram (see Figure 7). For this you will need five tumbled stones (1–5), ten single-terminators (6–15), and your catalyst crystal. You should prepare for the healing in the same way as described in the earlier configurations. Then place one tumbled piece of quartz crystal (stones **1–5**) at each point of a large pentagram around the body (see Figure 7). Now place the single-terminated Quartz points in this order: **6** – above the head and **7** below the patient's left hand, pointing along a straight line from stones 1–3. **8** below the left knee and **9** above the right hand, pointing in a straight line from stones 3–5. **10** outside the right arm and **11** outside the left arm, in a straight line from stones 5–2. **12** above the left hand and **13** below the right knee in a line from stones 2–4. And lastly, **14** below the right hand and **15** above the head in a straight line from stones 4–1. Once all the crystals are in place, position yourself about two feet from the head of the patient facing down their body. Visualise the pentagram. Then begin channelling energy through the first crystal and slowly down through the body and toward the patient's left foot. Visualise the energy bouncing off of the stone beneath the left foot and up to the stone at the patient's right shoulder, travelling through the lower base energies. Again, visualise bouncing it off the crystal at the right shoulder, across the chest and heart, to the stone at the left shoulder. Now 'push' the energy down across the base energies towards the stone beneath the right foot. Finally, bounce the energy back up towards the 'pinnacle' stone above the head.

This cannot be hurried and, with experience, you will notice that where energy centres are clear, the flow will be consistent. Where there are blockages, the energy lines will 'drag' and slow down. Sometimes there is a feeling of speed and you might find it hard to control the direction of the energy flow. This is often encountered where there is a sort of 'whirlpool' of energy, spinning erratically out of control. Just persevere. On each circuit you will experience greater control over balancing the overall pace of the energy flow. Everyone has a different pace and you must try to attune to theirs – and not impose your pace on them.

Once you have spent a while doing this you will aware of the vibration from each main chakra. If you decide that there are some that need additional help, place the corresponding crystals directly onto the centre. If you need to speed the centre up, use a crystal that has a faster vibration like Citrine or Moldavite perhaps. This will work naturally and not force the bodies own resources. I like to use a piece of Tourmalinated Quartz for this – you'll quickly discover what works best for you. If you need to slow the centre down, I would use something like Agate, Jasper or a piece of Smoky Quartz. I also like to use Moonstone for this because it is feminine and cooling.

Once these are in place, go back to your original position and sit quietly watching over your patient. If the patient has the time, you might allow the crystals about 15 minutes to work by leaving them in place and working your way around each point in turn. Spend a while watching over the grid of energy you have placed in motion. When you feel the time is right, slowly remove the crystals you have placed on the body and feel the energy with your hands to see how effective the healing has been. You should notice a change in only one session, but your real purpose should be to feel if the energy centre still takes more heat from your hands. This is the only way I can positively gauge how much progress we have made and how many sessions are likely to be required. I realise that it is not always possible for some people to find the time for healing – but often, one session is like taking just one tablet from a course of antibiotics.

The 'Star of David' configuration

I use this configuration (see Figure 8) for balancing the polarities of male and female energy and also the physical and spiritual bodies. It is capable of pulling the two together to balance each other and work as one. It can be used on shy, timid people to aid their self-assertion when the female or negative side of a personality is dominant. Or, equally, on strong aggressive types who's male, or positive side is dominant, to calm and balance their energies.

It can also be used on a patient who is deeply distressed and suicidal. When the stress level rises it can feel that you may as well give up, and many in this state turn to drugs or bingeing on foods or alcohol for comfort. They prefer to live in a state of illusion rather then face reality and so spend their time on the astral plane where they feel free from physical restraints and their consciousness floats around in the ether. This is when they shut down their ability to feel, their emotional centre, under the illusion that this will protect them from pain.

This type of healing must be handled very carefully because sometimes the patient has erected many barriers and they are reluctant to remove them for healing as this would make them vulnerable again. Prepare for the healing as usual and then place six single terminator crystal points in the shape of two triangles. The first goes from top to bottom and the second goes bottom to top (see Figure 8). The first triangle is the male or positive polarity. Grounded and physical, it aspires and struggles towards the source – so the triangle points upwards. The second triangle is the female or negative polarity, employing intuition and a greater awareness in its perception of the larger picture. This needs to be perfectly grounded to create a balance and so the point of the triangle faces down. Place all the points of the crystals inwards and then, with your catalyst crystal, go over the outline of the triangles one at a time – first male then female. Repeat this about four times each, visualising the triangles in place. Then sit back and watch over your patient for about fifteen to twenty minutes while the crystals and the configuration do their work. Now remove the crystals and feel the energy centres with your hands over the body. Finish the healing as before, making sure the patient has thoroughly grounded before they leave.

This configuration is also known as the 'Twelve-Tribes' symbol and is believed to have been created by King David to symbolise the twelve tribes of Israel. However, the emblem is also associated with Solomon – and is an integral part of the 'seal of Solomon'. A point in the centre followed out to each angle of the star gives twelve individual triangles. It is believed that each tribe held one piece of esoteric knowledge. When mankind has achieved the level of understanding necessary, the twelve triangles become one and, as one united race, we will understand and share the knowledge of the mysteries. I have also heard it said that the two main triangles making the 'star' represent the forces of good and evil – and the collective whole symbolises the day of reckoning when Azazel and his followers are taken for judgement before God.

9

Cleansing
crystals

Crystals and minerals are formed deep within the Earth.
Obviously, by the time a crystal arrives in your possession
for you to work with, it will have encountered – and been
contaminated by – the many various energies that make up
'man'. In order for you to begin working with your crystal you
must first cleanse it by grounding all the energies, both negative
and positive, that it has picked up on its way through the many
hands from the mines to the crystal shop. This cleansing is
crucial. What is required from the crystal is the sacred, true and

uncontaminated vibration of unconditional love that crystals radiate naturally. Therefore, before working with your new crystal – offer it back to the Earth Mother. Through returning it to her care she will absorb and disperse any pollution it may carry. Then, when you bring it back from the Earth, wash your new crystal thoroughly – at the very least under the cold water tap. If it's at all possible, wash it in a running stream or, best of all, take it to the seashore and cleanse it in the powerful energy of the waves. Salt water is believed by many to be the very best method of cleansing because it contains the matrix of the feminine principle, i.e. matter. The molecular formation of salt is cubic. The cube is the fundamental geometric form representing the element of earth which is matter and water is the quality of the holy spirit, or soul, because of its fluidity. A word of caution. Soft crystalline structures can find salt water abrasive and this can alter the feel of the surface. Most crystals, however, will not have their properties affected. Some minerals, like Gypsum, are not suitable for washing. Check with your crystal shop if you're unsure. As a guide, Selenite, Malachite, Gypsum, Celestite, Lapis and Turquoise – in their natural state – I would not recommend for washing.

There are two main schools of thought when it comes to cleansing crystals for personal use. I must admit I have heard hundreds of intellectually valid viewpoints as to which is the correct procedure and, naturally, each believe theirs to be the right way. Having listened to both sides of the arguments, let me give you an insight into each and allow you to judge for yourself.

The first is to take the crystal into the garden or into nature. If that isn't possible, a window box filled with soil in will suffice. Gently scoop out a shallow hole with your hands (never use a sharp blade for this) and lay the crystal into it. Cover it with a little earth and note the spot. Leave for at least three nights before unearthing and rinsing off the soil. If you feel intuitively that your crystal has undergone trauma, maybe used in negative circumstances etc., then as a rule I personally place it in the earth for one Full Moon cycle. Your crystal is now ready for you to work with.

The second school of thought would appear to be the complete opposite. It is that crystals need to be exposed to the energies of the Sun, out of the womb of the Earth and born into the light. The rays of the Sun energise the crystal and it becomes the last transformation before effective human contact takes place. Crystals are placed in the garden, sun lounge or on window sills to soak up the solar energies. It is believed that this warms the crystal up and awakens its hidden powers. The Sun acts as the catalyst that clears and dissipates any negatives accumulated upon the matrix of the crystal at the hands of mankind. When the solar energies have done their work you should, again, wash the crystal in a source of running water. Exceptions to this are Amethyst and Rose Quartz whose colour will fade dramatically.

My own view is that these two 'schools' are not really that far from each other. If we have accepted the notion that the cosmos is really a flowing 'river of energy', then a crystal would be energised and cleansed from any exposure to that cosmic flow. I believe that both Sun and Earth are constantly bathed in this flow and, therefore, either would be a good source of its cleansing powers.

I find that the crystals that come into your possession have an exact attunement to your human energy field and act as a reflection of the inner-self or soul. For this reason it could be equally correct for one person to use the Sun while another uses the Moon to cleanse their crystals. We are all either Sun-based or Moon-based depending on the time of our birth – which also means that some are both Sun and Moon based. This may seem strange, but all it really mean is that each of us play a part in making up the balance of the universe – yin and yang. Many feel an affiliation to the positive driving energies of the Sun, living their lives as busy achievers who measure their success by the accumulation of material gains – by enjoying hours in the Sun soaking up the power of the huge golden orb. There are just as many whose affiliation lies with the Moon. They come alive in the small hours with brain activity. The writers, the thinkers and philosophers, the watchers of the planets and the ones who measure their wealth by the 'fewness' of there needs. These are Moon-based. Then there are those who border the two, they swim in the energies of both the Sun and the Moon, depending on their emotional surges.

For these reasons, Moon-based people attune to the energies of the Moon and would be drawn towards using the Moon and the Earth to cleanse their crystals – whilst Sun-based people prefer the solar energies and would be drawn towards using the Sun to cleanse theirs. Both would be right – right for them.

Using a pendulum for cleansing

Another way of cleansing crystals is by the use of a pendulum. Hold your pendulum a few inches above the crystal you want to cleanse. Ask that you be 'allowed' to cleanse the crystal. At this point the pendulum usually responds with a 'yes' response. Obviously, if the response is negative that crystal is not for you. Begin to channel positive energy, drawing it through your body and directing it toward the crystal. The pendulum will usually start to swing in a circle, gathering momentum. Allow the crystal to dictate the time required necessary to totally remove any negativity. I have seen pendulums swing casually and methodically – round and round calmly – and I have seen them swing erratically at considerable speed, turning the hand completely over in doing so. Ask me 'Do I believe that this is a good way to cleanse crystals?' In truth if this is the only option, as when the crystal is to heavy to move or if you need to cleanse a crystal quickly, then yes I believe it is not only a good way but also very effective.

Geodes as cleansing tools

Cleansing crystals with a Geode can be a gentle and peaceful experience for the crystal. Place it within, or in front of, a large Geode or surrounded by smaller Geodes. These act like nurseries to cleanse and heal them before they come into your care. A Geode can act like a generator that energises smaller crystals and minerals, allowing them to attune naturally and correct any imbalances in their vibration. They would need a few days to adjust before use and the Geode makes a wonderful tool for keeping all your crystals cleansed and ready for working with when they are not being used.

Ways of the elders

Some native American elders I have spoken to say that the only way to cleanse crystals properly is to make a pouch. This should be made of natural fibres with a drawstring closure. The crystals for cleansing are then placed in the pouch and held down in a natural running freshwater stream by a large boulder securing the drawstring. They should then be left for one Full Moon cycle before use. In our busy modern lives away from nature this could be considered a minor problem. However, it is also a reminder of how far away from nature and natural living we have really travelled.

10
Self-protection and karma

Now is a good time to talk about protection. If you have persevered this far then you should go no further without some knowledge of protection. Probably, your first question will be – 'Why do I need it? If I believe that nothing or no one can harm them, then surely nothing can?' If only that were true! We can buy almost anything with money – indeed money becomes an energy itself. It can buy bolts, barricades and bullets. It can buy insurance and we can insure against just about everything. Everything that is except the protection of our soul.

I am not writing this to alarm anyone or to appear a know-it-all. I simply need to share with you information which, in fairness, you have paid for by the purchase of this book. Another 'exchange' of energy. Psychic protection is about taking care of one's spiritual body which, as we have discussed, has a direct reaction on the physical body. Whilst learning the arts of channelling, meditating and healing you have learned to open up – little attention is usually paid to closing down. The reasons for this are obvious. Esoteric knowledge is at last coming 'out of the closet'. Consciousness has taken a huge leap forward and, today, any serious student of the mysteries can find the answers they seek. It was only in 1951 that the 'Witchcraft Act', which carried the death penalty, was finally repealed – and many forms of alternative healing would have come under that Act. Now, via the internet, television, books and workshops, it is possible to suffer from 'information overload'. This could be viewed as the positive side. The negative side is that, as in many things, materialism has reared its ugly head and there is a lot of money made out of spiritualism. The word 'occult' conjures up ideas of 'black magic' and, when added to talk of psychic protection, the media look for a story. That is not good business sense and so everyone tiptoes around the subject leaving the innocent vulnerable. A little information can be extremely dangerous.

With crystal healing, as in most forms of spiritual healing and meditation, you are shifting your state of consciousness. This, by its very nature, creates space. 'Ask and you shall be given' may seem a simple concept – but do we really understand it's implications? If our 'cup' is full, how can more be poured into it? It cannot. Therefore, in order to receive, we must first 'give'. To give away something of value will allow something of value to be received. As we open up our consciousness to the 'source', we take our spiritual body out through the chakras to join with the great 'flow' of spirit in the universe. This creates a space for pure energy to flow in, replenishing life force and healing the physical. It also allows for the experienced healer to channel this energy and use it for a higher good. While we are opening up and creating space we are becoming more sensitive and this can leave us exposed and vulnerable. The light of a being's soul burns like a bright candle. It can burn so brightly that darkness is attracted to it, and encroaches around to try and extinguish the illumination. But, however difficult the journey, you should never hold your light low or try and cover it. Always hold it high to light your footsteps – remember that life is a balance and where there is light there must also be darkness. Don't make your journey harder by walking in the shadows. Life is a struggle for all who step out on the path to enlightenment. It challenges our sense of reality and all our perceptions are turned upside down. Everything we hold to be true suddenly becomes false, everything we rely on for our feelings of security suddenly crumbles and disappears. It is the great trans-formation. The acceptance of change – and the only security is no security.

As we journey forward it would be foolish to go unprotected. We would become a magnet to all the undirected psychic 'debris' hurtling around from inexperienced 'dabblers' in the occult. Furthermore, it would be dangerous and naïve to dismiss protection as unnecessary. Too many new healers seem to believe that if they walk only a 'white path', they will always be protected. This assumes that there is no connection between good and evil on the spiritual plane. As we know – that is totally wrong. Even the recognition of 'good–evil' or 'right–wrong' varies tremendously from one viewpoint to another. The spiritual plane contains only energy. The distinctions between the forms of that energy are purely human and so, for our own protection, we have to assume that there are an equal amount of 'evil' or 'good' energies. Every time we sleep our 'spirit beans' go wandering. Some of us remember our travelling and some of us don't. However, our 'beans' store the experiences and file them away for future reference. We constantly interact with the universe and everything in it and that means both 'good and bad' energies.

Firstly, let's deal with protection on a psychic level. This is often encountered totally at random. It's not directed at us, it just affects us because we are sensitive. For example, you are out browsing in a quaint little market town and come across something in an antique shop that takes your fancy. Intrigued, you buy it and take it home. A few days later you notice you have not been feeling too well and are suffering a number of headaches. By the end of the week you start to realise that you haven't been sleeping too well either, and start to feel generally out of sorts. The energy in your home does not feel good – you're nervous, edgy etc. Before you know it, your mind goes back to your find from the antique shop. Whenever we acquire something that has been owned by someone before us, we are taking home the energy of the previous owner – or owners. If we are sensitive, and that energy is strong, it will have an effect on us – negative or positive. It is all a matter of being aware and taking precautions. If it is a piece of clothing, wash it straight away to remove and ground the energy. If it is something that cannot be washed it still must be cleansed. Try using a pendulum or smudge it with a sage wand. Consciously, you can visualise 'wrapping' it in a bubble and flushing it with light. Then send the bubble back to the pervious owner dead or alive. Some people will leave items out under the Moon for the mother goddess to cleanse, or use a crystal to 'trap' the unwanted energy and then bury the crystal. Whatever method you use, the most positive thing one can do is be *aware* of it.

Another example is walking into a crowded place, like a supermarket. There may not be anyone in particular directing negativity towards you. Yet, by being open and sensitive, within minutes you can become a gibbering wreck. A hysterical child is screaming in a buggy, an old lady runs into your ankle with her shopping trolley and, as you fight your way to the checkout, the assistant calls out that she is taking her break and 'Would you move along to the next aisle please' – which just happens to have a mile long queue. All these things can have a tremendous effect on the aura and, in turn, on how you feel. There have been many times when I have gone without rather than face the assault course of a crowded supermarket.

If you are this sensitive there are a number of things you can do – after all you always have the power of choice. Before you leave home, place a 'cloak of protection' around yourself. Visualise a golden cape swirling around your shoulders. Visualise it loosely covering your head, to protect the spiritual body, and reaching down to cover your feet. Keep in mind that this is to contain your own energy and separate it from the contamination of others. Remember to take the cloak 'off' when you return home. If, when you arrive at your destination, you sense that the energies are too stressful, you can always turn around and leave. That's your responsibility. No one, nor situation, can ever have more power over you than you are prepared to give up.

Some people will wear a piece of shiny jewellery or tiny mirrors sewn into their clothes to 'reflect' unwanted energies. For others, a lucky talisman or charm is given the responsibility of their protection. All of these have one thing in common. They are empowered by thought and can work extremely well all the time that you believe in them. If conscious thoughts have been worked into an object, that energy will be attached to it.

We have already discussed the fact that emotions are powerful things and that they create an energy of there own. This energy, when consciously directed, has the ability to create negative or positive waves that can either cause the most miraculous wonders of healing or be equally destructive. If someone means you harm, and consciously sets about to cause you discomfort, movement takes place out in the astral plane. Awareness means to have knowledge but knowledge alone is not *wisdom*. Voodoo, as practised in Africa, Haiti etc., works on people's vulnerability. Their fear, or respect, for the witch doctor is often the most powerful 'magic' involved – and their own mind becomes an extremely effective weapon against them. Voodoo (or tokaloshe) dolls and 'death-day' cards work because their magic operates on two levels. On the physical level, by the appearance of the doll or arrival of the card, and on the astral, by the intentions consciously worked into the doll or card and directed at the victim's spiritual body. Many cultures have similar beliefs and it is always easier to talk about other cultures than our own. It is almost 'too close for comfort' to remember that the ancient beliefs of England are pre-Christian, pagan and were practised by members of the wiccan or druid beliefs.

Psychic 'attack' happens when one person malevolently wishes ill to befall another – but there are many inbetween levels of which, at one time or another, we are all guilty. Take for example the times a mother calls to her child 'Don't run around – you'll fall over' and, of course, the toddler falls over. Now the question is – would it have happened anyway? Or, did the fact that she externalised the thought increase the chances of it happening? How many times do we say something and then touch wood, a custom of grounding that suggestion before it goes out into the universe. How often has someone offended or upset you and, in a moment of anger, you found yourself thinking – 'I wish they'd leave me alone and drop dead'. Then afterwards, with feelings of guilt, you 'wrap' that thought in a bubble because you didn't really mean it. All these are cases when the psychic energy is let loose without due control for a moment until one realises what they have said and are then amended.

Prayer is, by definition, psychic channelling. It is a solemn act of paying homage, giving thanks and requesting our desires to be realised. They are then 'organised' into 'thought' strings and sent off into the universe. In the Lords Prayer the words 'Thy will be done' are included so as to incur no negative karma by imposing your will over that of the divine creator. However, if we truly meant it, we would not be asking for anything, but rather adopting a 'zen-like' attitude of *what will be will be.*

There are a number of things we can do to protect ourselves from forms of psychic attack but first we need to determine what level of protection is required and from whom. This can usually be decided by the symptoms you are feeling. Are you feeling nervous, a little 'frayed around the edges', headachey, quick-tempered, paranoid, tearful or depressed? These are all classic signs that your defences are down and you are being drained. Try to put aside a few minutes each day to work on yourself – say ten minutes each morning before you start the day. Seat yourself comfortably and be sure that you are warm and will not be disturbed. Close your eyes and allow any stray thoughts to wander through your head. It may take practice but, with patience, you will soon be able to release these thoughts and clear a space in your mind. Now pay attention to your breathing and gradually, on each intake of breath, imagine your aura pushing outwards – giving you more room to manoeuvre and your physical body more substance. On the outward breath, 'see' yourself exhaling all the impurities within that space. A good meditation for keeping the space clear that you have just created is to imagine placing a Copper coil around you in the shape of an egg. Start at the bottom under your feet and gradually swirl it up, allowing it to expand around the body. As you reach up above your head, let it become narrow again – leaving only a small gap at the top to keep you spiritually connected. The Copper coil will ground any negative stressful energies you encounter all day and, before you go to bed, you can reverse this meditation and remove it. This whole ritual will only take a short time but, performed daily, it will increase your ability to cope with the mundane. It will strengthen your physical and spiritual bodies and help you to balance stress.

If the symptoms are more defined than these, such as a feeling that someone is watching you – your concentration failing – your focus becoming blurred every time you try to read something. Things, especially electrical items, breaking down – forgetfulness – sleeplessness and nightmares – noticeable health problems. These are signs of a more conscious attack. These are signs of someone knowingly wishing you harm or misfortune and so your greatest form of defence is attack. If you know who it is, and it can be dealt with on a physical level, then that is the quickest way to handle it. Confront them with the issue that has caused the bad feelings and deal with it. If you do not know who it is or are not able to face them, then there are a few other things that you can do to stop the attack. Mirrors placed at doorways and windows return the energy to whence it came and so you can return intentions back to the person responsible – who could be in for a shock. The burning of cinnamon essential oil in an oil burner dissipates negative energy and, in time, will drain the attacker of their psychic energy. Placing pieces of Obsidian by the front and back doors will remove negative energy from visitors as they arrive, giving it back to them as they leave. Wash or cleanse all crystals regularly and burn incense or smudge to keep the atmosphere clear.

Thought forms are a very valid type of protection and by placing 'guardians' around your home you can be sure of being alerted when intruders arrive. One way to protect your home or car is to walk around it visualising a series of interlocking circles with protective symbols in them, all the way around leaving no gaps. The symbol could be a crucifix or pentagram perhaps. This forms a protective chain. As you 'draw' each one you should repeat a prayer asking for protection. If you get to a point where your concentration goes and you forget the words or become confused – you can guarantee that this is where the attack is coming from. It is crucial, therefore, that you persevere and use all your will power to complete the procedure as it is your weakest link.

It is hard for psychic energy to cross water and many people like to live near the sea or freshwater running streams for this reason. Most of us, however, do not have that luxury and have to make do with keeping a small dish of water by our bed. This is believed to absorb any paranormal activity. It must be flushed away each morning and replaced again at bedtime.

If you feel really vulnerable, a circle of salt around the bed with four dishes of salt water (one placed at each direction, North–South–East–West) will give protection while you sleep. It might be considered an old wives' tale but trees, planted by doorways and around the boundaries of a house, have been used for centuries as protection. Evergreens are considered good for this. The rowan tree or elderberry are seen around many old cottages. Oak and willow are also a good source or protection and used in groves. Herbs grown in the garden or window box are also used to keep negativity away. Garlic, hung in strings perhaps, is the best known. Basil, bay, clover, heather, honey-suckle, lavender, mugwort, peony, roses (with sharp thorns) and sage, to name but a few. Thistles are often encouraged in hedgerows for their magical properties, as are blackberries. During the growing and harvesting season the properties of these trees and herbs as defensive armour is apparent, but during the winter months, when the energies return to the Earth

Mother, they are utilised in other ways. The dried flowers, leaves, bark and roots are used to mix into incense and burned as an offering to the energies from which aid is requested or honour and thanksgiving paid.

Another old custom is to program large Quartz points to collect negative energies and then bury them point down in the Earth around an area you wish to protect. Five is a common number, which are then placed in the Earth on points describing a pentagram. Earth–Air–Fire–Water and Spirit, respect is paid one for each of the elements that make up the physical body – and one in recognition of the spiritual body. When placed around a home such a crystal formation takes all negativity to Earth. When placed inside a circle in the garden it makes a safe retreat to worship or meditate.

You may find some of these ideas extreme and if you never have cause to use them then that is for the better. However 'forewarned is forearmed' so keep them 'tucked away' in the back of your memory.

To finish on this subject, I have to say that probably the most widely used method of taking psychic care of yourself is be responsible. Remember to close your chakras down. Visualise each energy centre as an 'open' lotus flower. Concentrate on closing the petals on each of the flowers around their energy centre. When they are all closed, encircle each with a white light. This can be done at any time – anywhere and is very useful when you suddenly feel unprotected or vulnerable. It is an instant shielding.

Karma

This is a subject that I believe to have been designed to keep down the multitude. It conjures up figures like the Devil and uses them ruthlessly so that good 'followers of the faith' would never question it. I question everything. It is part of my make up and my conclusions are drawn from my theory of the 'human beans' concept. Try and keep the idea of the 'beans' in your head and follow this through. For every action in your life an amount of energy is used. If you perform a loving, unselfish deed – since 'like attracts like' – an equal amount of energy comes back to you. Performing a positive action means that, through your body and aura, a positive energy has been pushed out into the surrounding energy. Here it finds contact with positive calm and loving energies. Performing a negative action, for example an act of selfishness or violence directed at another for your own personal gratification, will hurl that emotion out through the aura like a huge ball that gathers momentum as it spirals out through the universe. Again, 'like attracts like' and at some point the ever growing ball of negative energy will come back, returning to whence it came. A person's energy has its own unique identification, made up from all the emotions they have ever felt. These stay attached to the aura through each of our reincarnations. 'Deja-vu' is simply one energy recognising another familiar energy. A feeling from the past of which the physical may have no recollection. This means that, depending on the ferocity of the energy expelled, that one negative outburst can take many of our years to return – but return it will! It does not matter that the person may have moved on or that they may even be in a different physical existence. This is not, however, the concept of one soul jumping from body to body. It is more a causal imprint of connection. It is not a 'different' person, but it is not the same 'soul person' either. I visualise it as similar to 'Newton's swing', a number of heavy steel balls suspended, from a frame, by a trapezium. When one ball is set in motion it impacts the next – then the next etc. The effect each time it strikes is similar but not exactly the same as the last. The initial energy that sets the balls in motion eventually dissipates and they return to a static position. But the energy pattern each time would be determined by the laws of cause and effect. The four forces relating to the motion being Thrust: element Fire, Resistance: element Water, Lift: element Air, Gravity: element Earth. As the atoms that make up the human body descend to Earth, gravity pulls them together and one becomes dense matter again but not the same make up as before. The beans are reshuffled so to speak.

Alas human nature that it is seeks justice in instant karma – to see one reap one's just rewards. It is easy to become judge, jury and executioner all in one careless minute, making yourself no better then the person committing the first negative act. The concept of turning the other cheek is seen as a passive response and thought of as a weakness in modern society. On a path of spiritual enlightenment we are taught love and forgiveness. Never to seek revenge and burden the heart with hate. I have found that the 'acceptance' of another's actions, as being their karma – for them to deal with, detaches me from collecting the 'baggage' of their karma while still allowing me to forgive the soul of that person. If that same person's actions are physically or mentally affecting me, then I have a responsibility to my physical and spiritual bodies to protect them and move away from the danger.

As the very nature of negative karma is active and aggressive, the 'threefold law of karmic return' is more likely to happen at a slower rate then positive karma because it would be thrown much farther out into the universe.

To tie these two important chapters together for the purposes of healing, we need to visualise going through the early stages of a healing. As we open ourselves up protection is needed so that only positive energy is channelled as we make the connection to source. Next, the homage paid to this source in return for your request is the exchange of energy required to keep a balance. And, lastly, remember that each has a karmic past and it may be that the person 'asking' for healing is not yet ready to receive it. They may still have lessons to learn on their path and the illness may be part of that lesson. (They may not be ready to empty their 'cup'.) Therefore, as a healer, you do not want to take on another's karma, just to help them where you can. To protect yourself you should always mentally ask: '*if it be karmically possible*' may you be allowed to be used as a channel for healing.

Thy will be done and not my will be done.

11

Crystals
and
the stars

Solar and planetary influences

In one twenty-four hour time frame the Earth turns once on its axis, during which time the Sun, Moon and planets each rise and set. Ancient astronomers noted that within this movement in the pattern of the heavens, approximately every two hours a symbol was recognisable. These periods became known as the signs of the zodiac. Approximately every twenty-eight days the Moon travels through one of these astrological signs in a certain order and, as it does so, various angles are made in relation to the other planets. These angles are called aspects and each aspect has influence over our life, either negative or positive, depending on our date and time of birth. In conjunction with this, the skies are also divided up into what are commonly known as houses. These are the ascending signs on the Eastern horizon at the time of one's birth and are associated with characteristics. Each zodiac sign is also associated with an 'elemental' force, either Earth, Air, Fire or Water, three signs for each element. There is, in fact, a fifth element which permeates all the other elements and that is Space. The element of energy is directly related to our nature and the shifting of our awareness, allowing us to understand these traits and face them.

Earth

Earth sign people are hard working, physical, grounded, practical and slow to change. The neurotic element of the Earth aspect would be to accumulate unnecessary possessions, achievements, friends etc., the illusion of security. This, transformed, would be the ability to make a home out of anything, a stillness and satisfaction of the moment.

Air

Air sign people are mentally agile. They are quick thinkers and communicators, usually managing to get others to do their bidding while they plot. They are in constant motion. The neurotic element of air is its grasping side, its speed and paranoia. It would, in reality, be too fast to perceive things as they really are. This transformed would be the ability to move spontaneously and appropriately in the moment.

Fire

Fire sign people are energetic, quick tempered, forceful and assertive. They love to win and are strongly driven by passion and desire. The neurotic element is the need to consume – not to collect but purely for the satisfaction of consuming. This transformed would be perfect unity without the need to seek or devour. Instead, they would radiate warmth and show discriminating wisdom.

Water

Water sign people are known for their natural compassion. They are intuitive but sometimes struggle to gain control over their emotions. They are normally passive and often taken advantage of but, when they are pushed to their limits, they can be capable of extreme opposites. It is true to say that Water can put out Fire. The neurotic element could manifest as anger which, like frozen ice, can often have a precise cutting quality. This transformed would be perfect clarity like the reflective quality of still water – a mirror-like wisdom.

Space

The fifth element which permeates all signs and all elements would be Space. It is like the centre of the medicine wheel but in reality this 'centre' is everywhere. In its neurotic aspect it would be dullness, boredom, stupidity and depression. This element transformed would be perfect openness, vastness and the Buddha nature itself.

Sign	From	To	Element	Symbol
Aries	March 21st	April 20th	Fire	Ram
Taurus	April 21st	May 21st	Earth	Bull
Gemini	May 22nd	June 21st	Air	Twins
Cancer	June 22nd	July 22nd	Water	Crab
Leo	July 23rd	Aug 22nd	Fire	Lion
Virgo	Aug 23rd	Sept 22nd	Earth	Virgin
Libra	Sept 23rd	Oct 23rd	Air	Scales
Scorpio	Oct 24th	Nov 23rd	Water	Scorpion
Sagittarius	Nov 24th	Dec 21st	Fire	Archer
Capricorn	Dec 22nd	Jan 20th	Earth	Goat
Aquarius	Jan 21st	Feb 19th	Air	Water Bearer
Pisces	Feb 20th	Mar 20th	Water	Fishes

The Sun sign dates, elements and symbols are listed above. The dates are approximate and vary from year to year due to the solar year not being exactly 365 days.

We do not yet know enough about how crystals, gems and minerals relate to the signs of the zodiac, but we do know that qualities attributed to them align themselves naturally and are able to aid our health once this connection is made. What we have learnt, over the years, is that it is not simply a matter of acquiring and wearing the complementary crystal or mineral associated with our zodiac sign. In fact it is more likely be true that the crystal associated with your opposing sign is a more relevant one. This has proved the case in situations where someone's nature is classically relevant to their elemental sign. For example, someone with the zodiac sign of Pisces, with their ascendant sign also being a Water sign, would probably get little or no benefit from wearing or using Amethyst. Amethyst, because of its energy, would only exaggerate the existing qualities of Pisces – potentially creating an even bigger imbalance than the person was already struggling with. They would derive greater benefit from Carnelian or Sugilite, associated with their opposite sign – Virgo, so restoring the balance of physical, emotional and mental stress. To make identification easier, I have constructed a reference table. It relates each of the zodiac signs to precious and semi-precious crystals and minerals with their elemental energy and direction.

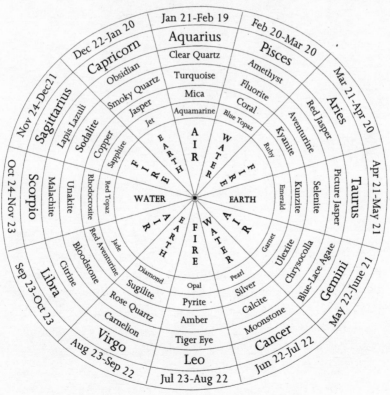

Figure 9   Crystals and their zodiac associations

12

DNA of
the Earth

Crystals and minerals contain all the elements of Earth, Air, Fire and Water within their make-up and, as such, are the very DNA of the Earth Mother herself. Through many transformations they are eventually ready to embrace the element of spirit. The energy field of a human is of a higher vibration, as is the animal kingdom of a whole, and our metabolism is much faster than that of a crystal. This doesn't mean it is better or purer. It is just faster. The 'crystal kingdom' has the ability to aid the spiritual evolution of mankind and, in so doing, it will automatically aid the spiritual evolution of the Earth Mother who mankind has repeatedly obstructed through his own wilfulness and greed. We live in a beautiful world and it has managed to stay that way for millions of years only because no one can actually take anything away from it with their death. We can use the Earth's resources, manipulate the Earth's resources and move the Earth's resources around. We even destroy and pollute the Earth's resources – but we cannot take any part of her with us into the afterlife. As we journey to the spiritual realms we are clothed only in the 'raiments of the soul'.

Crystals and minerals are the record keepers of time and space. As such, they come to us as miniature 'power houses' or libraries waiting to be accessed by another intelligence, one that is able to attune to the sensitive energies encased within them. When our awareness has evolved to the point where we can 'read' the matrix of the crystals, like the tiny 'memory chips' of a computer, we will be able to retrieve the information placed there. Some believe that such information could have been placed there by the Creator Himself in order to save mankind – if only from himself. We are at a significant point in our history right now. As time seems to accelerate our evolution, we reach the point where, as a species, we can achieve virtually anything. The problem seems, to me, to revolve around the moral issues. We have become so preoccupied with the fact that we *can* perform these scientific feats – we have forgotten to ask if we *should*! Our lack of humility staggers me at times and I cannot resist looking back to the dawn of our knowledge as I try to 'see' the future we will leave to our children. Man has been here before.

When mankind has advanced enough to be able to create 'in his own image', that is the very time he will need to remember the fate of the 'Watchers' (or 'Fallen Angels') who the Guardian Angels – Gabriel, Michael, Uriel and Raphael – were called upon to discharge, according to the 'Book of Enoch'. Perhaps the knowledge held within special crystals was placed their by the Archangels themselves. The book tells us that special knowledge was shared with mankind to aid and protect him. Not the most sacred but some of the great mystery. Where else on the planet could such knowledge have been hidden, in such primitive times, except within crystals? And to protect mankind from what exactly? Fallen Angels, aliens or could it be ourselves?

> Thou seest what Azazel hath done, who hath taught all unrighteousness on earth and revealed the eternal secrets which were (preserved) in heaven, which men were striving to learn. And Semjaza, to whom Thou hast given authority to bear rule over his associates. And they have gone to the daughters of men upon the earth, and have slept with the women, and have defiled themselves, and revealed to them all kinds of sins. And the women have borne giants, and the whole earth has thereby been filled with blood and unrighteousness. And now, behold, the souls of those who have died are crying and making their suit to the gates of heaven, and their lamentations have ascended.
>
> **The Book of Enoch. Chapter VIII. 6.**
> **Translated by R.H. Charles**

The spiritual evolution of mankind, according to the writings of Enoch, was threatened drastically as tormented souls gathered in the lower realms – unable to progress. Negative energy built until, eventually, an imbalance occurred causing the need for the Earth Mother herself to intervene. The distress signal was reached, on the astral plane, for the pure energy of source to send down the 'Guardians' to cleanse the Earth. The Earth was cleansed, by the great flood, for forty days and forty nights (or so we are told). Storms raged, killing all life on Earth except Noah and those safely housed in the ark.

It is easy to judge and condemn the 'watchers' or 'gods' or even alien intelligence for corrupting mankind and interrupting our spiritual evolution. For causing negative karma, or perhaps blaming them for creating the 'missing link' that has eluded science for so long. We search for 'who' or 'what' was responsible for the anomaly of our past. In fact we search everywhere – except within ourselves. Wouldn't it be the most wonderful thing to genetically engineer another species from our own DNA – a creation 'in our own image'. Just for a moment, contemplate the advantages of having endless supplies of human organs for transplant and experimentation. To be able to perfectly clone only the genetically healthiest and strongest of mankind – to live only long enough to be useful. There would be no point in having them live past there 'sell by date'. Make them male and female in order to reproduce without continual scientific support. Give them just enough capacity to think and reason to fulfil our basic needs. Make them content to be subservient to us, the 'master species' and replace the need for us to do the mundane troublesome jobs that take us away from our leisure. Take away the instinct of emotion, there will be no need and indeed they will be less trouble without the problems of rivalry, passion and temperament. Content to 'man' our space exploration plans of the future – bringing back untold knowledge of our galaxy without the risk to human life. Now what have we achieved, a species genetically engineered to make our lives safer and easier, who look upon us as gods fulfilling their every need . . . But what if something unexpected happens? In time, even while we are enjoying our leisure idly watching over our creations, we would become increasingly bored. Eventually, the full realisation of our achievement dawns and our attention is drawn to the beauty of this new species of ours.

Perhaps more so because they are so willing to obey our every whim – looking up to us as their mentors and saviours to whom they owe their very existence. Before long the immoral lust contained within the dark side of the human psyche can no longer be contained and the immortal sin is committed, resulting in the 'birth' of a cross species over whose behaviour we have no control. The offspring of this unholy union have the strength of Hercules and minds of their own. Born out of the negative behaviour of man, they hold within them the exaggerated nature of all our darkest aspects. Soon they take the planet by storm, creating havoc and mayhem. With no morality or responsibility they become unstoppable. They are huge, ruthless beings, half man – half animal consuming everything that breathes. The voices of the innocents cry out unable to rest in the realm of the dead and unable to progress past the negativity brought on by their brothers. The archangels respond to their call. In consultation with the 'great source', the angels are despatched to save the mother goddess, the planet Earth. Her charges, the caretakers of the planet, have proved unworthy and their fate is determined. They shall burn in the eternal fires of damnation along with their hideous mutations. The Earth burns, the seas boil and all is destroyed. Thick black smoke screens the Sun, darkness presides and all life is laid waste. Many years pass. Then, one day, a spacecraft lands. Two people emerge and step out onto a barren land. Gone are all the familiar things that were in abundance when the couple left many years before. Gone are their mentors and security. Gone are their schedules and duties. Returned from the mission that has taken many years of their lives they find they are left to face the future alone. As they look to the sky a slim beam of sunlight breaks through the smog and kisses the ground in front of their feet. Following the shaft of light, they notice a tiny green shoot unfolding its head from the soft earth beneath. Adam takes Eve in his arms to comfort her and for the first time a stirring deep inside awakens a memory deep within the subconscious – and emotion is born.

Imagination and pure speculation? Or may it hold more than an element of truth? Whatever your answer, you have to admit – it certainly sounds familiar . . .

Index

Sub-headings to crystals and ailments give additional information to that in the main entry shown in bold.